CUSTOM HOME &
HOME ADDITION ADVISOR

CUSTOM HOME &
HOME ADDITION ADVISOR

AN OWNER'S GUIDE TO Planning, Pricing and Supervising a custom home or home addition project

VERN WESTFALL

CUSTOM HOME & HOME ADDITION ADVISOR
AN OWNER'S GUIDE TO PLANNING, PRICING AND SUPERVISING
A CUSTOM HOME OR HOME ADDITION PROJECT

iUniverse books may be ordered through booksellers or by contacting:

iUniverse
1663 Liberty Drive
Bloomington, IN 47403
www.iuniverse.com
1-800-Authors (1-800-288-4677)

Because of the dynamic nature of the Internet, any web addresses or links contained in this book may have changed since publication and may no longer be valid. The views expressed in this work are solely those of the author and do not necessarily reflect the views of the publisher, and the publisher hereby disclaims any responsibility for them.

Any people depicted in stock imagery provided by Getty Images are models, and such images are being used for illustrative purposes only.
Certain stock imagery © Getty Images.

ISBN: 978-1-5320-9257-2 (sc)
ISBN: 978-1-5320-9258-9 (e)

Print information available on the last page.

iUniverse rev. date: 01/21/2020

Use The Custom Home Advisor Guide to prepare yourself
- Use the information in *Managing a Custom Home Project*, to choose the best approach and to prepare yourself.

Use The Custom Home Advisor Guide to locate and engage a Project Advisor
- Use the information in *Using a Construction Advisor*, to locate, evaluate, and contract with an experienced Advisor.

Use The Custom Home Advisor Guide to prepare the project
- Use the *Design and Planning Calendar*, to shape the design and to measure your design and planning progress.

- Use the *Design, Planning and Pricing Guides*, for the information you need to design, plan and price efficiently.

Use The Custom Home Advisor Guide to oversee and manage construction
- Use the *Construction Calendar*, to schedule and, with the help of your Construction Advisor, control the construction process.

- Use the *Construction Oversight Guides*, to manage effectively, optimize site visits, evaluate financial interfaces, and to keep accurate records.

Use The Custom Home Advisor Guide to make the process easy
- Use the *Reference Section*, for help in reading blueprints for help in making calls, for essential checklist and forms, and for help in organizing your files.

CONTENTS

PROJECT MANAGEMENT

DESIGNING/PLANNING AND PRICING

CONSTRUCTION

REFERENCES

PROJECT MANAGEMENT

MANAGING A CUSTOM HOME OR
HOME ADDITION PROJECT

In an owner-managed custom home project, the owner's oversight responsibilities are similar to those required when building any new home. Custom homes require only an additional emphasis on planning and preparation.

When the mass production of automobiles made the automobile affordable, cookie-cutter home production also became popular. Before mass production, nearly all new homes were custom homes. After mass production, suburbs developed around cities and new neighborhoods became duplicate home designs built on small plots. Companies like *Aladdin Homes* and Montgomery Ward's, *Wardway Homes*, began offering mail order home kits in the 1920's. Older neighborhoods reflect this period of home construction. Newer subdivisions with restricted design offerings continue the trend. For developers and builders it remains easier and more profitable to limit design options than to allow creative new designs. As a result, similar designs make up the bulk of new homes built in the United States, but the demand for truly custom homes persists and is a growing part of the new home market.

This guide addresses the growing custom home market by offering owners an approach to managing their construction project without becoming an expert in new home construction, and can save owners tens of thousands of dollars. The approach offered by this guide also offers general contractors a lucrative way to assist and advise owners using their construction expertise without assuming the liabilities associated with standard general contracting arrangements.

USING A CONSTRUCTION ADVISOR

This guide introduces the *Construction Advisor* option, illustrates the savings and advantages of owner managed custom home projects, and describes the responsibilities of a *Construction Advisor*.

By transferring contractual responsibilities from the general contractor to the owner, the general contractor becomes a *Construction Advisor* and their services become affordable.

In *Owner-Financed / Owner-Controlled* custom home projects, owners assume similar liabilities and spend only slightly more time overseeing the project than they would in a more standard general contractor arrangement. This guide simplifies the owner / contractor interface for both the owner and the contractor.

OWNER CONTROLLED CONTRACTING

PART 1
MANAGING YOUR DESIGN / BUILD PROJECT

PROJECT MANAGEMENT

Choosing To Be Involved

Planning, pricing and overseeing a custom home project involves many material components and many labor specialties but, with help in locating essential tradesmen and by using a construction advisor, project oversight and management is well within an owner's capability. Owners can oversee and coordinate the planning and construction of a custom home with ease by simply turning to the section matching their project's progress and following the guides. Project calendars keep the project on schedule while project checklists keep the project on track.

Home designers have the expertise to design a custom home and general contractors have the experience needed for construction oversight, but neither may want, or be capable of, managing the project, and neither has the vested interest of the owner. Owners are deeply involved in the custom home design-build process regardless of the role they choose. Even when owners abdicate all oversight responsibilities to the designer and the general contractor, they will still ……

- be responsible for design and planning decisions
- provide essential oversight
- make separate building site inspections
- make the same number of selections
- sign the same number of approvals
- track and approve the same project expenditures
- deal with the same delays and problems

Owners have two options. They can be an active participant in the planning, pricing and construction of their new home or they can engage and pay a general contractor to manage and control the project. This guide can serve either role. For those who choose to engage a builder or general contractor, the guide will make them a more effective partner in the design-build process. For those that choose to assume a more active management role, but are uncertain of their ability to deal with building inspectors and tradesmen, a general contractor's advice and experience can be made affordable by contracting the general contractor's services as a construction advisor.

A Construction Advisor is a general contractor with a limited management role.

Construction Advisors defer to the owner in making important decisions, but provide advice and oversight as needed. Following the job description in this guide, a general contractor becomes an experienced advisor engaged for a reasonable fee instead of a large percentage of the projects total cost. Many builders and general contractors prefer this more limited role because it limits their scheduling and financial liabilities. Hired only as an advisor, the general contractor concentrates on quality and compliance instead of scheduling and accounting and can answer on-site questions and spot discrepancies the owner might miss. A competent construction advisor can also help deal with building inspectors and sub contractors when questions arise. The qualifications, responsibilities, restrictions and a suggested compensation plan for a construction advisor are included in part two of this section. A suggested contract is included in Reference Tab 6.

Owners should base their choice between direct or indirect management roles on money, not time. Even when an owner gives the designer and project manager complete control, the owner will spend as much time making selections and anxiously monitoring progress and approving expenditures as they would with a direct management role

An owner-managed project builds equity by reducing oversight and material-handling costs, by avoiding secondary financial charges, and by avoiding hidden markups associated with a general contractor's relationships with suppliers and subcontractors. Active owner management creates owner equity earnings of $75 per hr, or more. On a $400,000 home, an owner-managed project can reduce costs and increase equity by as much as twenty percent.

Making meaningful contributions during the design process and assuming additional scheduling and accounting responsibilities during construction, requires less time than one would think; approximately ten hours per week during planning and pricing and approximately eight hours per week during construction is usually sufficient.

Owners should choose which approach is better for them based on their willingness to accept additional responsibilities for project finances, for placing construction material orders, and for contracting with and scheduling subcontractors. Most project activities will involve the owner regardless of management arrangements. By assuming additional roles in their project's planning, design, pricing, and construction, owners save much more than they can by engaging in labor-intensive roles.

Owners willing to exchange anxious observing hours for active project oversight will invest an average of nine or ten hours a week for one year. By being actively engaged in planning and oversight, owners can reduce costs by 20% or more. Some of these savings come from providing oversight during planning and pricing, the rest comes from reduced management and liability overcharges. To create these savings, owners need to participate in the planning and design process, make pre-selections, and establish relationships with subcontractors and suppliers early. "Home Advisor" and "Angie's List" can play an essential role by providing contacts for home designers, vetted tradesmen, and builders or general contractors willing to work as construction advisors.

The Home Construction Industry

Residential construction has job descriptions and titles with multiple meanings. It is easy to hire a builder when you really wanted a project manager or to hire a carpenter when you really wanted a builder. Another term with multiple meanings is *developer*. A developer is generally an investor who purchases and develops land by adding streets and utilities and then parcels the developed land into building sites. Often however, the developer is primarily a builder who holds all or some of the building sites hostage to promote their building business. Other developers recoup development costs early by selling purchase options for some of their lots to carpenters who have decided to become builders. You see their signs on optioned lots in many new subdivisions. The message these signs send is, "I paid to advertise here so deal with me if you want to build on this lot."

Production builders approach construction using standard models and few design changes because they do not want to deal with complex pricing and a long and complex customer interface. Avoiding confusing definitions and poor price forecasting methods is important in the construction of any new home but is critical in a unique one-of-a-kind custom home project. It is especially important in custom homes designed and built under the control of their owners. With proper advice and guidance, owners can oversee their own project, save money, and enjoy the process.

(1) Custom homes need not cost more than standard models if managed properly.
(2) With guidance, most owners are capable of managing custom home construction projects with ease.
(3) Mistakes during design, planning, and pricing are often more expensive than mistakes made during construction.
(4) Building site conditions can affect the cost of design and construction significantly.

All new home construction projects involve planning, pricing and supervision as key elements. A tract homebuilder avoids these key demands by using the same plan repeatedly, by building the same or very similar homes many times over, and by having the same tradesmen repeat their efforts home after home. Modifications to a standard plan that require pricing and supervisory adjustments are discouraged. This type of standardization creates the similarity of homes in most of our existing neighborhoods.

This guide addresses the *custom home market.* It guides the owner through the same key elements of planning, pricing, and supervision, but from a different perspective. A custom home cannot rely on previous projects to provide a plan, an accurate price, accurate material lists, or repetitive labor costs. As a result, the process is always a new endeavor and planning and building requires a well-planned and organized approach.

A custom home starts with only a collection of ideas. As a result, planning and organization require even more attention. The following guides are not about the details of pouring footers, framing, or applying siding. Experienced tradesmen can provide these skills and bring their experience to a project along with a great deal of pride in their work. Local building inspectors provide quality control inspections as a part of the permitting and approval process, and reputable material suppliers offer special services for customers with large projects. Bringing these, labor, material and quality control elements together requires planning, oversight, organization, and careful accounting. The guides that follow bring these elements together in an easy to follow, "step-by-step" process.

Providing essential oversight is not difficult if a systematic approach is used. Planning and supervising a custom home project is not as daunting as it seems and, if one remains organized, requires less time and less effort than one would expect. The secret to a successful custom home project is to spend an equal amount of time <u>planning</u> and in forecast pricing, as in final bidding and construction. Every detail resolved in planning and price forecasting eliminates a future question or mistake and becomes an instructional moment that prepares the owner for construction oversight. Plan and price well and you have, in essence, built the home before you start construction and, like the tract home builder, are prepared by experience for construction oversight.

Unfortunately, there is a tendency to hurry through essential first steps by working with inappropriate purchased plans, or by assuming that a lumber and foundation bid is sufficient to establish an approximate total cost for the project. This rush to feasibility creates many future problems. It alienates those who spend a great deal of time preparing a bid, or a material list, only to be approached later with a modified plan and asked for another bid. It leaves out the bulk of essential pricing elements required for an accurate cost estimate and, by being a cursory effort, fails to educate the owner and fails to identify and eliminate problem areas that carry forward to permitting and construction.

Every hour spent planning and pricing in the comfort of an indoor setting saves many hours in the wind and mud trying to find a solution to an avoidable oversight. Thorough planning and pricing saves tens of thousands of dollars by presenting clear and complete information to bidders and suppliers. It also creates contacts and relationships that become invaluable during final pricing and construction. A poorly planned or poorly presented project creates pricing-pads, overbids, and a grapevine reputation among subcontractors and suppliers as a dangerous project.

To be effective you need to design in detail, plan well, and price accurately. This takes time and effort and demands close attention. If you are not ready to purchase a building site, are not ready to oversee and fund the effort to produce a complete and detailed blueprint, or are not ready to break the plan down into its many pricing components and make preliminary selections for price, you are not ready to start creating a new custom home. You can continue to gather ideas, search for a building site and prepare yourself emotionally, financially and educationally, but the actual design, planning and pricing process should be postponed until you are ready to commit and continue.

To be effective as a project manager you need to avoid any temptation to put details aside until you start building. You need to complete every step, follow every guide, and fill every blank. To design, plan and price effectively you need to prepare yourself and the project thoroughly and position the project for maximum savings and minimal problems. Make the effort now and your new home will cost less, be much easier to build, be completed sooner, and be a positive experience. This guide is useful only when applied fully during the initial phases and only if you follow the detailed planning and pricing guides.

Preparing for the Experience

You are about to make your dream come true, literally. From your ideas, a new home is about to be designed and constructed that will fit your life-style, meet your needs, and accommodate your likes and dislikes. There will be limitations and compromises but overall you will structure the dream.

Before a designer can transform your ideas into a set of plans, you need to transfer your ideas to the designer visually and verbally. Begin by going through home plan magazines and by taking pictures of existing homes. Don't expect to find the perfect plan or house; it rarely happens. Instead, circle the exterior and interior features you like and don't worry about selecting conflicting ideas or disagreeing with your spouse. Some of the best design features are the result of a compromise between seemingly irreconcilable preferences.

Compromises may be required between your design and your budget and between your design and your building site so keep your expectations real. Indoor pools and sports courts are possible but; if your budget can't accommodate these luxuries, don't put them on your wish list. To communicate effectively with your designer, put your magazine clippings and photos into a portfolio with notes attached explaining why you like the highlighted design features. Another good way to communicate your likes and dislikes is to take your designer on a tour of your existing home, pointing out what you like and dislike.

As you collect ideas and envision your new home, think beyond the immediate. You will probably live in the home you are planning for ten years or more and things will change. Your family will grow or shrink. older relatives may move in, children may move out. Plan primarily for *now* but keep the future in mind and don't forget pets and serious hobbies. As you dream, expect boundaries. Building codes impose restrictions as do structural limitations, energy considerations, etc. Some restrictions are obvious some are not. The planning guides that follow will help identify limits and restrictions.

While you collect and discuss design ideas, consider how you will adjust your personal schedule to accommodate your upcoming project responsibilities. If you will be sharing the planning, pricing, scheduling and bookkeeping responsibilities with a spouse, the job will be much easier. The demand for ten or so hours per week during the five-month planning phase will require more self-discipline than the eight or so hours per week during the seven-month construction phase. Do not neglect the planning phase! It shapes the new home, its construction, and determines its cost.

With site selection, planning, and pre-selections complete, your construction advisor will begin to assist with subcontractor selections, pricing, and construction oversight, allowing you to concentrate on your primary obligations, scheduling, finances and final selections. If you have planned well, have been serious about making (pre-selections for price), and have established working relationships, in advance, with suppliers and subcontractors, the seven months of construction will run smoothly with few problems.

Setting the Tone

Keep the big picture in mind and the few problems you encounter during construction will seem small. An unavoidable delay caused by a supplier, tradesman, or the weather may frustrate you, but if you keep a positive attitude, the project will continue in a positive manner. You, along with your construction advisor, set the tone for the work and the attitude surrounding your project. You need the tradesmen more than they need you. Don't let them get away with shoddy work but always compliment them for a job well done. Bring them coffee and doughnuts, ask questions, offer their family tickets to an event, etc. but don't show favoritism. Never loose your temper and approach every delay and problem as a temporary set back capable of resolution through cooperation.

Dealing with Delays and Problems

In a custom home project, a dozen or more tradesmen are required to assemble hundreds of materials supplied by dozens of suppliers in an outdoor environment. It is a somewhat convoluted process and things won't work perfectly. Most delays and glitches can be resolved with a phone call and the few that can't, will be resolved with the help of building inspectors, your subcontractors, and the construction advisor.

Life is not perfect, especially when it gets complicated, and you may need to make a compromise that bums you out. Everyone hopes this doesn't happen, but if it does, look for something special you can add somewhere else and let it go. Don't allow a small compromise to ruin your attitude by dwelling on it, or by repeating the story to family and friends. Problems make good stories but, even after being resolved, become the first things your friends will look for when they inspect your completed home. Say nothing, and oversights and compromises will go unnoticed, and you will quickly forget them.

During the construction phase of a custom home project, owners expect suppliers to make deliveries on time and sub contractors to show up and complete their tasks in a timely manner. Owners need to do the same during the planning phase. The planning and pricing phase is the easiest to ignore or rush through, but it is the most important part of the project. Think of the time you spend in planning and pricing as both project preparation and as management training for your upcoming responsibilities.

Keep accurate records, follow the guides, and measure your progress. Pre-construction efforts create the most equity. Every penny you save by planning-ahead and planning-well becomes equity in your completed home you can use later to lower your construction loan or borrow against to send your son or daughter to college.

Commit to the Project

When you decide to search for a building site or think about adding on, you make a partial commitment to planning and building. When you actually purchase a building site or decide to build an addition, you are ready to begin architectural design work and fully commit to the project. By announcing your project and making commitment investments, you separate the project from your other activities, focus your attention and let suppliers, contractors, and lenders know you are serious.

To commit to your project:

- *Give your project a name*
- *Open a bank account for miscellaneous project expenses, separate from your construction loan.*
- *Separate project mail from your personal mail by using a PO box or by making it a new resident at your address.*
- *Purchase a separate "project only" cell phone with a separate number. Start taking project photos.*
- *Purchase or designate a notebook or laptop computer for project records and e-mails. Establish a project e-mail address*
- *Start to keep a daily log of activities, expenses, contacts, mileage, etc.*

If you are unwilling to risk a thousand dollars to prepare and organize yourself to manage your several hundred thousand dollar project you may want to wait until you are ready to commit fully. When you are ready, a good way to announce your commitment is to host a commitment party with family and friends.

OWNER CONTROLLED CONTRACTING

PART 2

USING A CONSTRUCTION ADVISOR

CONSTRUCTION ADVISOR	Options
CONSTRUCTION ADVISOR	Job Description
CONSTRUCTION ADVISOR	Responsibilities
CONSTRUCTION ADVISOR	Restrictions
CONSTRUCTION ADVISOR	Compensation
CONSTRUCTION ADVISOR	Qualifications

THE CONSTRUCTION ADVISOR OPTION

Most custom home projects still involve a general contractor but owner managed projects are becoming popular and construction lenders are becoming amenable to funding owner-managed projects. Unless you have construction experience, the choice between turning your project over to a competent general contractor or managing it yourself is daunting, but there are tens of thousands of reasons to consider the construction advisor option.

General contractors mark up the price of a custom home to cover liabilities, their financial involvement, planning and pricing efforts, scheduling responsibilities, overhead, profit, and for the headache of having an anxious owner looking over their shoulder for seven months. General contractor markups can be 25% or more. Owners can save the expense of a general contractor by managing the project themselves but, without a guide or construction experience, choosing to go it alone is frightening. Fortunately, there is a fourth option, a middle ground that brings the construction expertise of a general contractor to the project without their usual markup.

There are four management options for the planning pricing and construction of a new custom home.

1. A builder managed modified model home
2. A general contractor managed project

3. An unassisted owner managed project
4. An owner managed project using a construction advisor

Examine the options and make a decision. The "Custom Home Advisor" guide is applicable to any of the four options

CONSTRUCTION ADVISOR JOB DESCRIPTION

Given the right guidance and support, almost anyone is capable of managing the planning and construction of a new custom home. Owners shy away from the opportunity because they lack the practical construction experience of a general contractor. Builders shy away from contracting custom home projects because of financial liabilities and unwanted organizational responsibilities. Custom homes have a difficult overlapping management interface between the owner and the contractor. Both owners and general contractors are responsible for expenditures. Both owners and the general contractors share responsibilities for selecting and acquiring numerous specialized materials, and must coordinate decisions regarding project scheduling.

The "Construction Advisor" approach separates and simplifies the tasks of the owner and the contractor by specifying and separating their responsibilities. By eliminate the confusing overlap the owner becomes the project planning and scheduling manager and the general contractor becomes a construction advisor. The Design / Pricing and Construction sections of this guide detail the owner's responsibilities. This section details the construction advisor's responsibilities.

Construction Advisors are local builder/contractors with extensive experience in residential construction and general contracting. They are often semi-retired general contractors, mom and pop builders, experienced past custom home project managers, or designer builders.

Construction Advisors work with the owner under a formal agreement. The work is part time, requires an open schedule, and allows for other work as long as it doesn't interfere with their advisory responsibilities. A general contractor can continue work on other projects as long as they are able to meet their contract obligations.

Unlike standard general contracting responsibilities, construction advisor responsibilities do not include the liabilities associated with full project oversight. A construction advisor's responsibilities are limited to giving good advice, helping to solve problems, and offering encouragement and support. A construction advisor consults and advises owners primarily on matters related to construction, job progress, scheduling, quality of materials, quality of work, and construction related problems.

The following is a general overview of a construction advisor's responsibilities. There are limits for involvement and on making critical decisions, but as anyone ever involved in construction knows, the list of unexpected situations is endless. A good construction advisor will assist and advise the owner-manager in best methods, help solve problems, and help avoid delays without making decisions for the owner.

CONSTRUCTION ADVISOR RESPONSIBILITIES

During the late stages of the planning phase, construction advisors assist the owner-manager in reading blueprints, evaluating prospective subcontractors, evaluating material suppliers, evaluating bids, and by providing guidance in obtaining permits. Construction Advisors can also assist owners in locating specialty tradesmen and in locating sources for unusual or hard to find materials.

During the construction phase, construction advisors will establish an early rapport with owner selected subcontractors and suppliers and explain the role of the owner as the project manager and their role as advisor to the owner and quality control inspector.

Construction Advisors must be available for building site inspections during working hours, for phone consultations and available to meet with the owner at least three times per month. These meetings can occur during regularly scheduled construction advisor building site inspections, or at other locations and times.

(See "Owner/Construction Advisor Agreement" in Forms, Tab 6)

Construction Advisor responsibilities include meetings, inspections, consultations, and three building site visits per week to inspect work-in-progress. Using their own cell phone, they are required to take photographs of deliveries, correct any sub standard work, note work in progress, and alert the owner to materials needed. After each site inspection, the construction advisor forwards photos to the owner's project phone along with text observations, problems, and suggestions. Any serious conditions or situations require a verbal notification.

(*See* record of Construction Advisor Site Visit, Tab 6)

Construction Advisors provide their own transportation and travel as needed within the local area to meet with owners, make building site inspections, and for other reasonable travel in support of the project. To keep accounting simple, a mileage allowance is included as part of the construction advisor's monthly payments and is not be tracked.

Construction Advisors will talk to subcontractors and suppliers on a regular basis to asses the status of the project, be aware of any problems or needed supplies, pass on or clarify the owner's instructions, and arbitrate misunderstandings when requested by the owner. construction advisors resolve problems without usurping the owner's authority.

Construction Advisors do not have all the answers, but are expected to help solve problems, find answers, offer good advice, act professionally, and remain honest.

CONSTRUCTION ADVISOR RESTRICTIONS

The owner makes all final determinations as to the acceptability of a construction advisor's "other work responsibilities". The owner can establish additional restrictions for other obligations and include them in the Construction Advisor Agreement as needed.

The construction advisor will not accept any payments or gifts from suppliers or subcontractors for overlooking sub standard supplies or poor work, for promotion for selection by the owner as a subcontractor or supplier, or for any other compensation from suppliers or subcontractors related to the owner managed project not specified in the Owner/Construction Advisor Agreement.

The Construction Advisor will not subordinate duties or contract requirements or assign any duties to other persons, companies or organizations. The Construction Advisor will immediately notify the owner of any situation or condition that interferes with or impedes the performance of their contracted duties.

CONSTRUCTION ADVISOR COMPENSATION

The following is a suggested compensation schedule.

Compensate the Construction Advisor for **part time** services at a rate of $800 per month during the final two months of the planning phase and at a rate of $1,500 per month during the seven-month construction phase.

Additional compensation

- Approved additional construction site inspections with reports, (three per week are required by contract), $100 per additional visit.
- Additional meetings with the owner or others requested or approved by the owner, (three per month are required by contract), $100 per additional meeting.
- Additional telephone consultations and conference calls initiated by the owner, (two per week are required by contract), $25 per additional call.

Begin regular Construction Advisor payments after the Owner/ *Construction Advisor Agreement, (Tab 6)*, has been signed and as sub contractor and supplier selections begin.

The issuance of a building permit will mark the end of the planning phase and the beginning of the construction phase. Continue regular monthly payments for the duration of the project.

Make a final successful project completion payment of $1,500 after the issuance of an occupancy permit, negotiate any needed extensions of the Construction Advisor's compensation beyond the anticipated seven-month construction period, and recognize an early completion with an appropriate bonus.

Compensate the Construction Advisor for any assistance and advice needed after project completion at the additional meetings rate of $100 per consultation.

CONSTRUCTION ADVISOR JOB QUALIFICATIONS

Posses a strong background in residential construction management or related residential building trades, (on site construction-management experience preferred, total project responsibility experience desired).

Be willing to work under contract as a 1099 independent contractor with no benefits, and have sufficient income from other work to justify a 1099 position.

Possess the ability to work alone without constant oversight and supervision.

Be able to read and understand residential construction blueprints and specifications.

Be experienced and capable of dealing constructively with diverse tradesmen and subcontractors.

Posses basic mathematical skills, be able to operate a computer and have an e-mail address, posses and be able to take and send photos and text messages using an "I" phone.

Possess basic writing skills and be able to communicate clearly on complex construction related matters.

Be able to keep accurate records and ordered files.

Be personable and be able to work well with professional clients.

Be capable of working with construction material suppliers, numerous sub contractors and building inspectors in a calm and logical manner to resolve misunderstandings and to negotiate compromises.

Posses reliable transportation and be willing to travel frequently to the job site and the owner's home and occasionally to other local locations and businesses on matters related to the Project.

qualifications 1 of 2

CONSTRUCTION ADVISOR JOB QUALIFICATIONS

CONTINUED

Be capable of climbing and traversing difficult construction site conditions.

Be free of allergies and health conditions that would interfere with outdoor or indoor visits to construction sites in bad weather or where dust and construction dust and debris are present.

Be able to answer questions related to blueprint interpretation and various construction methodologies. Be able to resolve construction site difficulties and differences of opinion by offering sound advice and logical solutions.

Be able to help Owners keep their anxieties under control and their delays and difficulties in perspective.

Be able to remain calm in argumentative situations and when their expertise or honesty is questioned.

Be willing to admit ignorance when a situation arises that is outside their experience. Be willing to seek answers from reliable outside sources for the owner and sub trades when needed.

qualifications 2 of 2

DESIGNING/PLANNING AND PRICING

PART 1
DESIGN AND PLANNING

DESIGN and PLANNING CALENDAR

Month One

Find and secure a building site
Collect and organize design ideas
Examine funding options
Choose a designer/architect
Set up project files
Establish a project accounting method

Month Two

Begin formal design work
Interview potential Construction Advisors
Locate potential subcontractors
Locate potential construction materials suppliers
Choose a basement type
Begin initial preliminary selections
List essential contacts

Month Three

Approve the preliminary design
Select a Construction Advisor
Continue preliminary selections
Continue search for sub trades and suppliers

Months Four and Five

Approve the final design

Months Four and Five continued

Solicit labor and material bids
Final selection of subcontractors and suppliers
Arrive at an accurate forecast cost
Secure financing
Contract with selected sub trades and suppliers
Obtain permits

USING THE DESIGN AND PLANNING CALENDAR

Single-family residential construction projects, large and small, follow similar paths from concept to completion. Design / build projects add complexity by requiring hundreds of choices. There is no reasonable way to force a custom home or home addition project into a perfect schedule. Problems and delays are unavoidable but can be minimize by:

1. Planning and preparing thoroughly
2. Making personal selections early
3. Avoiding unnecessary changes
4. Resolving problems quickly and calmly

The Design and Planning Calendar provides a reasonable timeline for readying a custom home project for actual construction. Read and follow the cursory comments in the calendar and refer often to the more detailed instructions for completing each calendar element in the associated guides.

Follow the expanded calendars and guides that follow and you will be ready for construction in five months. Concentrate on the one and two month periods detailed in the expanded calendars one at a time. Be through, do not jump ahead, complete each segment and refer often to the checklists and forms in "References".

DESIGN AND PLANNING CALENDAR

MONTH ONE

Find and secure a building site
Collect and organize design ideas
Examine funding options
Choose a designer/architect
Set up project files
Select a project accounting method

NOTE: Do not, clear, work on, or park anything on your building site, without your bank's approval and a building permit.

Find and Secure a Building Site
(See "Locating and Evaluating Building Sites" in Tab 1)
(See Building Site Evaluation Checklist in Tab 1)

If you have already secured a building site, guidance for evaluating building sites may seem unnecessary, but your site will limit and dictate many facets of your design and the same criteria used to select a building site also applies to shaping your design to fit an existing site.

Some of the building sites you examine may come with an attached builder. One way for builders to attract customers is to develop land and then hold the lots hostage. Another way for builders to attract clients is to secure purchase options on several lots in one or more newly developed subdivisions and then post their signs. Do not pass up these potential building sites until you have called and asked if the lot is available without the builder's services, or with the builder acting as a Construction Advisor. Tell the builder you will be building a custom home that will be an owner-financed project with you acting as the project manager but will need an experienced general contractor to assist you for a fee.

Where you build is just as important as what you build. Where you live will adjust your life style just as much as your new house will redefine the way you live. The building site will also determine what you can build. Take your time and select carefully. The following considerations should help you organize your search.

The general area of a building site search is usually determined by work, family, access to schools, or shopping, and by a desire for a specific immediate setting, such as a subdivision, a country lot, or acreage. To organize your search and to assist others who may be helping you, establish a search area and list your preferences. Use the "Planning and Pricing Guides" in the next chapter to locate and evaluate potential sites.

The design process is an essential part of project planning. It should also be the most fun, but there are restrictions. Your building site will dictate some of the design elements by the slope of the land, view, and sun angles, by access or approach limitations, by neighboring structures, trees etc. Building restrictions and building codes will also play a part in creating the design with set-back restrictions, side yard limits, sewer depths, and neighborhood building restrictions. These imposed design limits along with your families needs and desires make thorough planning essential.

(See, "Locating and Evaluating Building Sites" Tab 1)

Collect and Organize Design Ideas

To begin, collect and assemble a small portfolio of design ideas. As you look through house plan magazines, do not try to find the perfect design. Finding a perfect design is unlikely. Look for design aspects you like, not a complete design. When you see an attractive window style or porch or bathroom layout, circle it. Make a list of what features and what rooms you want and note interior arrangements that are important to you. These lists and design aspects need not be compatible with each other or well ordered. Your family and life style is unique and a good designer can assemble most of your desires into a functional attractive whole.

If you have a definite plan in mind, look it over closely, there are always small adjustments that can improve the design. Do not try to arrive at a final design unless you are familiar with building codes, structural requirements and have secured a building site. Initial meetings with home design experts will allow you to ask questions, get free advice and select the designer you want. At this point, your dream home is mostly ideas, pictures, and bits and pieces of plans, but these cursory efforts have begun to structure the dream, establish design limitations, and create alternate ideas.

There are three basic approaches to securing a design for your new home:

1. Select a builders basic model or standard design

2. Locate an existing design in plans books, on line etc.
3. Engage a professional home designer.

A search for a suitable custom design usually involves all three approaches. If you have been anticipating this project for some time you have probably already collected numerous ideas. If you have been touring models and going through plan books, you have learned that the variety of designs and design possibilities is nearly unlimited. Homes, like people, are unique and each has their own character. Even cloned homes with cookie cutter architecture soon take on a distinctive character as their occupants decorate and modify them. If you are using the services of a professional designer you may be modifying an existing design or creating something unique. No matter how you begin, your final goal is a complete set of acceptable blueprints.

The following hints may speed up the process.

- As you search on line and through magazines, do not search for the perfect design. You will probably not find it, but if you do, stop searching and concentrate on your selection. If you keep searching, you add doubt about your perfect selection with every new interesting idea you see. Add up enough doubts and you are back to square one and are buying more magazines and starting over. Instead of just flipping pages and eliminating every plan that is not perfect, get out your pencil and start circling parts and pieces of designs that attract your attention. Circle the portion of the plan that got you to look a second time. Write down why the feature attracted you and mark the page. You may still find a perfect plan but if not, you will have a list of features and ideas that will guide your designer when you start the design process.

- Searching for components and features, both exterior and interior, organizes your thoughts and should help define your ultimate goals. An exception to this is a team search by husband and wife. A two-person search will inevitably run into incompatibilities. When this happens, view the conflict in design preferences as an opportunity, not a problem. Quite often two different points of view can create a compromise that is better than either alternative.

- If you find a design that seems to need only slight modifications to fit your ideal design, mark down the changes you want and get help before you get excited. Even an apparently simple modification can sometimes alter many other design features and twist your perfect choice into a not so perfect selection. Always look beyond the floor plan at exterior elevations and rooflines. A finished design is always a compromise between structural limitations, exterior and interior appearance and a desired floor plan.

- When you engage the services of a professional designer or architect, let them know if you are open to suggestions, and keep no secrets. If you are anticipating a relative moving in later, tell the designer. A designer may think of a walk out basement as additional living space that should be open to space above, but if you want these areas separated by doors and closed stairways the designer may design in error. If you want the drawings to follow certain ideas, let them know. An unwanted professional effort to improve your plan can cause delays and doubts.

Examine Funding Options

There are two separate investments associated with building a custom home: (the land, and, the house). One approach is to purchase the land and use the equity in the land as a down payment to secure a construction loan. Another approach, offered by some financial institutions, is to combine the property loan with a construction loan. Both loans roll over into a more standard mortgage when the house is finished. There are many types of financial institutions and many types of residential construction loans. Guidance from a financial advisor is advisable.

The structure of a construction loan can negatively affect the ability of an owner or contractor to make timely payments to subcontractors and suppliers. Some construction loans put residential construction projects in jeopardy by requiring a large deposit to secure the loan and then delay disbursements until a significant part of the project is completed. Delays in disbursements to cover acquired costs force the owner, or general contractor, to make additional out of pocket payments to avoid mechanics liens.

This dangerous deficit condition occurs when loan conditions limit disbursement to completions of major phases. An example is withholding a first disbursement until the foundation is complete, has been inspected by the local building department, and approved by a banking inspector. With each inspection, building department and bank, taking up to two-weeks, and with deposits and payments for framing supplies due in advance, a serious deficit condition can be created and require outside funds to avoid mechanics liens. Payments due before the lending institution will disburse funds are common in this type of arrangement and puts the project in a late payment status from the beginning. Starting in an arrears position can continue throughout the project creating delays, liens, and serious problems.

Owners should carefully examine the requirements for the disbursement of funds and weigh potential delays against other advantages the loan may offer. Discuss disbursement policies with the lending officer and use the Construction Calendar along with detailed pricing from quotes, bids and selections to forecast when payments will become due. A loan agreement that disburses funds upon the presentation of legitimate invoices works much better than disbursements based on stages of completion.

Choose a Designer / Architect

Home Advisor and Angie's List can refer architects and home designers in your area but selecting an independent home designer may be difficult. Many homebuilders claim the "home designer" title by using a simple computer design program to attract clients. The designer/builder designation should not eliminate them as a prospect if they are experienced in custom home design beyond a simple off the shelf computer program, and are willing to quote a separate design fee without claiming sole rights to the design. If found qualified both as a designer and a builder, ask if they might consider exchanging their usual general contracting position to be considered as a Construction Advisor. Beyond Angie's List and Home Advisor, seek referrals from custom homeowners, lumber companies, and local general contractors to locate experienced independent home designers. Off-the-shelf home design programs are not capable of creating an accurate and complete set of construction blue prints and professional computer aided design programs, (CAD), require extensive training to be useful and accurate. Perfect lines and corners by a computer do not make house plans professional or accurate.

Choose your designer carefully. The *first purpose* of your completed drawings is to satisfy you, the owner, that the design meets your needs and desires. The *second purpose* is to satisfy the building department that the design meets codes, is structurally sound, and meets energy requirements. The *third purpose* of completed drawings is to provide an accurate, to scale, presentation for use by suppliers in determining materials needed, and an accurate guide for assembly for use by tradesmen.

By agreement, architects do not advertise, however, they are easy to locate because they list themselves in the yellow pages. In general, the larger the architectural firm, the more they concentrate on large commercial projects, the more they charge, and the less interested they are in designing single family homes. Architects fees follow industry standards and are usually considerably higher than that of an independent home designer.

Your house plans will serve several purposes:

- They will present your ideas as a formal description of what is to be constructed
- They will be used by suppliers to estimate the materials needed to build the house
- They will be used by sub trades to bid labor costs and assemble the materials
- They will assure building inspectors of conformity with building standards
- They will be used by lending institutions to determine an appraised value

Who can legally design a single-family home?

The first thing you are looking for in a designer is experience in residential design. In most States, this need not be a registered architect. In most States you, the owner, may also design and draw your own plans as long as they are complete, are drawn to scale, and accurately depict the house to be built but, unless you have some experience, an inexpensive computer design program will not be enough to produce what is required.

What is the difference between an architect and a home designer?

Many architects are not experienced in residential design. An architects stamp is required to design commercial buildings but usually not to design single-family residences. Architects prefer commercial projects because they generate larger profits and have a less complicated client interface. As a result, not all architects are proficient in residential design and often apply commercial design standards to a residential project creating overly complex drawings and specifications. Overly complicated drawings create over bidding and over pricing. Vet architects, just as carefully as you would vet an experienced, but unlicensed, residential designer. The biggest difference you will find in house plans done by architects is detailed electrical, plumbing and heating drawings and lengthy verbal specifications. These detailed instructions are required for commercial projects but are usually not required, *or desired,* for residential projects. A preconstruction conference between the owner and mechanical contractors to mark up a set of plans for special heating, plumbing and electrical needs produces a better end-result and considerable savings.

Detailed plumbing, heating and electrical drawings are generally not required for residential designs and when included are rarely followed and drive up bids. Mechanical sub trades, (plumbing, heating, and electrical), require special licensing and separate inspections during construction. Most mechanical subcontractors are capable of planning and specifying and must meet code requirements. They will also advise you, without charge, and help you with special requirements.

Ask to see blueprints and actual homes done by the individual or firm you are considering. Ask questions and, if possible, speak to past clients. You will need a personal rapport with your designer that gives you the assurance that he, or she, has the time to listen, is listening, will charge a flat fee, (is not charging by the hour), and understands your desires.

You also need assurance that the designer can interpret and present your ideas in a way that complies with codes and requirements and, can be understood by residential tradesmen. Every custom home is unique and very few reflect a pure style of architecture. The designer you choose may be "well known" for a particular style of home, but if you want something more eclectic, you need an assurance that he or she is capable of breaking away from their established approach. Some designers will design on a computer screen and then enlarge the drawings to meet scale requirements. Some will design using drafting equipment and a pencil. Both will produce acceptable designs and drawings but the cost of their design services can vary greatly. Use common sense and choose using your best judgment. Computer aided designs have no advantage over pencil drawings done by an experienced designer.

Set up Project Files

(See Tab 4)

Start keeping track of everything related to your custom home project immediately. Most will become tax deductions. Include your early efforts to find a building site. Include dates, travel, mileage, and related expenses. If you have neglected to record your early efforts to find a suitable design including touring model homes, magazine purchases, and purchased plans, record them now.

If you have committed to your project, you have given your project a name, have set up a separate bank account for misc project expenses, and have established a separate mailing address to receive invoices etc. You should also have acquired a project cell phone for project correspondence and photographs, and have designated a laptop to keep track of contacts, expenses, and progress.

In addition to electronic files, a custom home construction project requires paper files. Purchase a large, (sales representative type), three ring binder, tab separators, and a three-hole punch. A detailed guide to organizing your paper files is included in "Guide to Files in References". The "Forms Section in references" also includes blank forms you will need to copy and use to record your preliminary selections for price, bids from subcontractors. Copy the blank forms you will need to record selections, solicit bids, deliveries and your site visits etc. Put them in your project binder along with important checklists and important agreements and contracts. Your binder will fill quickly as you add completed forms. Keep your original blank forms separate you will need to make further copies.

Set up computer oriented, project accounting and photographic files in advance. Being organized from the beginning will become essential when bidding and building become complex. Accurate financial files along with detailed progress records and photos will keep the project on schedule, within budget, and prove useful in resolving any disputes. Use the checklists and forms provided, and record keeping will become routine and easy.

Project Accounting

The accounting method you use to keep track of your custom home project is up to you. You can use a spreadsheet and a pencil or a computer program, but be aware there are several accounting anomalies unique to custom home construction. In addition to balancing the distribution of funds from a construction loan with payments for materials and labor, one also needs to determine the financial status of the project at regular intervals by balancing the forecast cost at various stages of completion against actual expenditures at that stage. One also has to account for miscellaneous costs outside direct expenses as well as overruns and unexpected savings. A balance of the "over and under" status of each construction element in, (labor, materials, and misc.) will offer a better status of the project than whole project expenditure percentages.

(See Tab 4)

DESIGN and PLANNING CALENDAR

MONTH TWO

Begin formal design work
Interview potential Construction Advisors
Locate potential subcontractors
Locate potential construction material suppliers
Choose a basement type
Begin selections for price
List essential contacts

Begin Formal Design Work

(See Reading Blueprints Tab 2)

During the initial design process, you have several very important tasks. You will be setting up your project files, searching for a Construction Advisor, making essential contacts, locating suppliers and sub trades, and making preliminary selections. Checklists and guides will assist you with these tasks. You will also be guiding and reviewing the actual design process. Suggestions follow.

Do not start design work until you are ready. If you keep searching for ideas while the designer molds your original parameters into a functional design you create a perpetual process. An occasional new idea during the design process is expected, but the interjection of an entirely new set of design standards after a major design effort has already taken place, may mean starting over and require additional design fees. Preliminary design work is essentially an exercise in communication with the designer interpreting the information provided by the owner and presenting it in graphic form.

When you searched through plans and magazines, you probably developed the habit of approaching each new plan by looking first for things you did not like. Approach the preliminary design effort differently. As you review your designer's efforts, look first for things you do like. The designer's goal is to include as many of your ideas as possible. The designer's first attempt may not satisfy all of your desires but should include most of them. Take the time to study preliminary attempts before coming to conclusions. Work with your designer. When your designer offers an alternate idea, examine it in a cooperative spirit. Try to understand why he deviated from your original plan. Good designers will not compete with your ideas and you should avoid competing with them. They are trying to guide you through the process and, If they stray from your vision, it is almost always because of a structural or regulatory restriction. If the designer's ideas have merit, put your ego aside and look for a compromise. If the designer has misunderstood you, gently put him or her back on track and apologize, even if it wasn't your fault. The process of building a new home is a cooperative effort from start to finish. Don't let egos or a competitive spirit sidetrack an exciting creative experience.

The first review of a preliminary design works best if the designer explains fully why they have arranged components of the design the way they did by pointing out how he or she tried to meet your ideas and how structural and other restrictions limited the approach. Take a day to review the initial design attempt before you have the next design conference. Keep the planning process in perspective. Remember that it is only an interim step. Your goal is a beautiful home, not a beautiful set of plans. Once the home is complete, the blueprints have little value beyond a ready reference.

Architects are trained to sketch and present preliminary ideas at a small, 1/8th inch per foot scale, but preliminary floor plans drawn to a larger, ¼" scale are easier for owners to read and avoid changes when scaled up. Ask your designer to develop preliminary plans at a ¼" per foot scale if possible. Preliminary house plans should include, in addition to floor plans, front, side and rear elevations, a basement outline, and a rough roof plan. When the designer is required to create these extra drawings, he is forced to think through structural details and avoid encountering a floor span or roof that is difficult or impossible to be framed.

There is no perfect design. Expect compromises, especially with structural necessities. Almost anything is possible but the nearly impossible can be very expensive. It is easy to draw a one-dimensional floor plan. It is not easy for a designer to create floor plans that are a compatible collection of structurally sound interior spaces supported by a structurally sound foundation and covered by an attractive and buildable roof.

Your new home will be only as good as the information and directions provided to those who build it. It is especially important to keep the design process in perspective. Elaborate computerized working drawings, beautiful renderings, and lengthy specifications are impressive but residential design presentations, when "overdone", create over bidding and price padding. Complex commercial style drawings can add confusion and expense by including unnecessary information, tables, references and specifications.

INTERVIEW POTENTIAL CONSTRUCTION ADVISOR'S

(Review *Part 2* of Owner Controlled Contracting and Reference Tabs 3 & 6)

Unless you are capable of managing the construction of your new home without assistance, you will need an experienced contractor/builder willing to act as your Construction Advisor.

While your designer works on the preliminary design

- build your project files
- begin making preliminary selections,
- make initial contacts with prospective suppliers and sub contractors
- locate and interview prospective Construction Advisors

To help in your search for a Construction Advisor search for independent builders and general contractors, use "Angie's List" and "Home Advisor", ask Lumber companies, and ask building departments, suppliers and subcontractors for referrals. You are looking for an individual with single family or home addition contracting experience, not a large developer-builder or contracting company.

The qualities you are looking for in a Construction Advisor are:

- Experience in managing custom single-family construction projects
- Availability with an open schedule, willing to work part time in a 1099 status with random hours
- Be willing to accept a flat fee for services and specific inspection and reporting requirements.

Construction Advisors are responsible for reviewing the owner's house plans, the owner's choices of subcontractors, the choice of suppliers, and for evaluating the building site. He is also responsible for reviewing the house placement and grade, (as set by the excavator or surveyor), and for making specified site visits during construction.

The Construction Advisor assumes no liability for errors made by others or for unintentional oversights. The Construction Advisor's job is to use his experience and expertise to identify and to bring mistakes, omissions or potential problems to the Owner's attention. The Construction Advisor is also required to meet regularly with the owner, and offer advice and intervene at the owner's request to resolve differences with suppliers, subcontractors, or inspectors. In general, the Construction Advisor will provide advice and assistance to the owner to insure a successful project outcome but will not manage the project.

The Construction Advisor is the most important selection the owner will make. Trust and compatibility are essential along with a strong commitment to the project. The owner is responsible for project accounting and financing, has primary responsibility for contracting and scheduling, (subject to the advice of the Construction Advisor), and makes all final decisions. Along with inspectors, sub-contractors, and suppliers the construction advisor provides construction expertise. A good working relationship is therefore essential between all members of the construction team and the owner must be willing to listen to their advice.

(See "Phone scripts Tab 3, "Interview Guide for Project Advisors")

Locate Potential Subcontractors

(See Subcontractors Needed checklist Tab 5)
(See Subcontractor Calling Scripts Tab 3)

During the design process, you should be, making preliminary personal selections, searching for subcontractors, evaluating suppliers, and making important contacts.

Do not release any preliminary drawings when you make initial contacts with potential subcontractors. Refer to the size of the house only in general terms, such as a large four bedroom two story home, or a small two-bedroom ranch etc. Do not use square feet. You are only talking to prospective subcontractors to see if they will be interested and ready when you are, and to judge their competency and honesty. You are only locating for potential subcontractors, not asking for prices. Get their phone numbers, ask for other referrals, and for any advice they are willing to offer. Use "Home Advisor", "Angie's List", your Construction Advisor, and local sources to find subcontractors. Build your files as you acquire names. You will make final subcontractor choices only after final working drawings are available and bidding is complete. Make no commitments before final working drawings are ready and bids are in.

Be aware that advice given by subcontractors during construction often includes an element of self-interest. Subcontractors tend to advise the owner to choose options that makes their job easier or less complicated. The owner should comply with subcontractor advice if the advice is good and if it does not negatively impact cost, the construction calendar, code compliance, or affect the work of other sub trades. Consult with your Construction Advisor and with your designer before making any changes.

(See Forms, "Change Evaluation" Tab 6)

NOTE: Avoid advanced unsolicited pricing estimates by sub trades and suppliers. Guesses based on incomplete or inaccurate information will influence final bid amounts. Make them wait for final drawings.

Locate Potential Construction Material Suppliers

NOTE: Construction material suppliers, (lumber etc.) are different from your personal selections suppliers. (Bathtubs, doorknobs, floor coverings etc.)

(See Material Suppliers needed Tab 5)

Use referrals from prospective Construction Advisors and subcontractors, Google, and the yellow pages to locate prospective construction materials suppliers, look for lumber companies. Build your files as you acquire names.

As you locate lumber and other material suppliers establish a personal contact, often a salesperson. They will have suggestions for windows, doors, trusses and specialty products etc. coordinate their suggestions with your designer. Let them know you are having a home designed and where it will be built. Let them know you are looking for a lumber and construction materials supplier that can submit a quote when the working drawings are ready. Do not release any preliminary drawings. Refer to the size of the house only in general terms such as a large four bedroom two story etc. Do not use square feet. Ask if they can supply doors and windows, trim materials, trusses etc. Make them wait for final working drawings. Use a single lumber and materials supplier if possible.

NOTE: Big box retailers are usually not a reliable source for construction materials. They are a good place to shop for Owner selected items but their employees generally lack the experience and expertise of lumber company employees. Large orders of windows, doors, etc. cause storage problems for retail stores, interfere with normal operations, and force deliveries to unprepared construction sites. When big box stores attempt to interface with specialized suppliers of engineered products, like roof or floor trusses, production, delivery, and storage problems are common.

Savings may occasionally override the disadvantages of purchasing construction materials from retail stores, but use caution.

(See Suppliers Needed Checklist Tab 5)

NOTE: For comparative purposes, big box material prices for lumber, shingles, insulation, drywall, etc. are available "on-line" and are a good place to find comparison prices. These become especially valuable if you have the time to calculate, or can obtain, independent material lists for your project. Being able to calculate the individual material cost in labor and material bids offers a check on over bidding.

(See Calculating Material Quantities Tab 7)

Choose a Foundation / Basement Type

There are several common types of foundations and many exotic experimental types. Not all meet building codes or get a building inspector's approval. The three most common and acceptable foundation types are:

- Concrete block walls on concrete footers
- Poured concrete walls on concrete footers
- Precast concrete walls on gravel footers

Concrete block foundations have been the standard for decades but are becoming less common as qualified masons become difficult to find. Advantages include low cost, and the ability to compensate for out-of-level footers and the ability to meet unusual structural and opening requirements. Disadvantages include special waterproofing requirements, difficulty in insulating, a requirement for an interior frame or wall for a finished interior, susceptibility to cracking, and longer construction times.

Poured concrete foundation walls are currently the most common type of foundation and have the advantage of moderate cost, strength, and, when reinforced and poured properly, are easier to waterproof. Due to the time required to build forms, the time required for constructing a poured foundation is only slightly faster than a block wall foundation. Disadvantages are difficulty in insulating, difficulty in correcting top of wall out-of-level mistakes, and requirements similar to block walls for interior finishing

DESIGNING/PLANNING AND PRICING

Precast concrete foundation walls similar to "Superior Wall" are becoming more popular in spite of their higher cost. Advantages include grade beam strength, ease in waterproofing, eliminating the need for a concrete footer, being partially pre-insulated, being installed by the manufacturer with guaranteed square and level conditions, being ready for additional interior insulation and drywall without additional framing, having better footer drainage, and needing only one day for installation. Disadvantages are a requirement for the basement floor to be poured and the frame floor above to be built, before any backfilling can take place. Higher cost are offset by shortening installation from weeks to a few days, by having the manufacture guarantee the basement and installation, by better strength and waterproofing, and by providing an insulation and drywall ready basement.

Begin Preliminary Personal Selections for price

(See "Items Requiring Owner Selection Checklist" Tab 5)
(See "Owner Selections Deadlines Checklist" Tab 5)

Even without a preliminary design in hand, you can begin to make preliminary selections. A garage door style, a front door style, siding types and colors, roofing materials and colors, cultured stone or brick facings, interior door styles, doorknobs, toilets, cabinet styles, etc. can all be made while your design takes shape. You have almost six months to make these selections but there are many of them and, if not selected in advance, they can delay the entire project. Some preliminary selections can be made on-line, others require show room visits. Copy the checklists in the Tabs and reserve a few hours every other week to stay ahead of design and construction. Keep accurate records

(See Checklists in Tab 5)

The contacts and preliminary selections you make while your design is in-progress will become an important part of your project files and will prepare you for final pricing and the construction phase of the project. They are very important; begin preliminary selections early.

The point of making preliminary selections is to:

- Prepare you for the many final selections you will need to make later
- To familiarize you with prices and supplier locations
- To build your essential contact list so you have the names and numbers you will need during construction

You are not making final selections. Many of the things you select may end up on your short list but, for now, you are only locating options and collecting preliminary prices and information. Every salesperson or clerk you talk to will push to see your preliminary plans and ask you to make a purchase. Let them know you will be making final selections later and ask them questions. Learn as much as you can about your preliminary selections and alternatives. As you wander the aisles taking notes, you may attract the attention of security. They are sensitive to competitors checking prices and offerings. Tell them what you are doing and will be making purchases when the house is in its final stages in about eight months. When you deal with a big-box kitchen design staff they will usually not design or price from house plans. You can get rough per foot pricing that may be good enough to forecast a cost for cabinetry and tops, but they will not design until the house is up with drywall installed. This can cause a serious delay. Independent kitchen cabinet suppliers are usually more accommodating but more expensive.

If you give a salesclerk your name, you can expect phone calls every few weeks to see if you are ready to make a purchase. Employees are required to make these follow up calls at regular intervals. You can't stop the calls without getting the employee in trouble so use restraint when giving out your contact information.

Keep a written record of every option, where you found it, prices, quantity discounts, colors, coverage, and if there are lead times for acquisition or delivery. Use your list of preliminary selections as a checklist to acquire final prices when your final working drawings are ready. Your preliminary shopping experiences will be of value, not only in providing a complete list of essential contacts, but also in educating and preparing you for scheduling during construction. NOTE:

(Use **only** final working drawings to make final selections)

List Essential Contacts

If you were diligent in evaluating your building site and used the guides and checklists provided you already have many of your essential contacts. Examples of essential contacts are, zoning inspector, health department officials, building department personnel, utility company contacts, neighbors etc. Enter all essential contacts *in your files and your project phone.*

(See Essential Contacts Checklist Tab 5)

PLANNING AND PRICING CALENDAR

MONTH THREE

Approve the preliminary design
Select a Construction Advisor
Continue personal selections for price
Continue search for subcontractors and materials suppliers

Approve the Preliminary Design

(See Reading Blueprints, Tab 2)

When revisions to your preliminary design reaches a point where only a few minor changes are needed, you should approve the preliminary drawings and give the designer the go-ahead for working drawings.

When you approve the designer's preliminary design, you are giving the approval to begin working drawings. The difference between preliminary drawings and working drawings is their purpose and number of detailed pages. The purpose of preliminary drawings is to satisfy you, the owner, that the house, as depicted, is acceptable without further major modifications. The purpose of working drawings is to provide details and renderings sufficient to guide suppliers in providing appropriate materials, subcontractors in assembling the materials, and building departments in assuring the design will produce a structure that is sound, functional and meets all codes.

- preliminary drawings should include complete floor plans to a ¼" scale,
- elevations of all sides of the structure in sufficient detail to allow a reasonable preview of how the house will appear when built,
- a foundation plan to a ¼" scale with all important dimensions and supports shown,
- A roof plan to a reasonable scale provides the owner assurance that the designer has considered the roof structure.

The owner's approval of preliminary designs is a commitment to the design as presented. It is not a temporary approval. It is an agreement that the owner will not introduce more ideas or changes that will significantly change the design.

Some changes, (after preliminary plans approval), involve changing only a label, (vinyl siding to stucco for example). Others, however, are much more difficult, (changing vinyl siding to real brick for example requires a brick ledge on the foundation and changes all the foundation dimensions. To avoid costly changes, cooperation between the owner and designer must continue as working drawings are developed,.

Working drawings, (in progress or completed), are presented and dimensioned in detail. Even a small change in the basic design can affect numerous details on many other pages. Tracing the impact of a late change to every detail on every page is difficult and often leads to oversights, conflicting information, and resulting construction errors. Unexpected changes, (after preliminary design approval), can also occur. These are rare but can occur from unexpected building site conditions or special building department requirements.

You have been working with your designer for at least a month and have gone through several revisions. You have probably made concessions to building codes and structural requirements but should be satisfied with the floor plans and the exterior appearance. After months and possibly years of anticipation and mental planning, approving the design for your new home is not an easy step. Reality has required compromises but the basic dream is now on paper, and if you are to realize that dream, committing to the drawings is necessary. Commit and move on to other important activities. Stop trying to tweak every little bit of the design. Concentrate on decorating by continuing to make important personal selections and by preparing yourself for construction.

It is ok to use preliminary plans as a personal guide for making preliminary selections during the design process but don't let a kitchen designer or someone at a pro-desk at Home Depot have them. Getting ahead of your approved working drawings will cause material shortages misfits and over pricing. <u>Preliminary designs "on the loose" are dangerous.</u>

SELECT A CONSTRUCTION ADVISOR

(Review Part 2 of "Owner controlled Contracting" and Tabs 3 & 6)

At a fourth the cost of a general contractor, a Construction Advisor can provide the expertise and oversight needed for an owner to manage a custom home project. Selecting a Construction Advisor is the most important selection the owner will make and the most difficult. The position of, "Construction Advisor", is not listed in the yellow pages or familiar in the home construction industry which makes recruiting difficult. "Angie's List", "Home Advisor", local homebuilders, building departments, and local subcontractors can offer suggestions and provide leads.

The position of Construction Advisor is not a suitable position for large homebuilders or contractors. It is best suited for a single person or small contracting firm or builder with a flexible schedule. Extensive residential building and contracting experience is essential. Construction Advisor is a part time position, Construction Advisors may continue with other obligations and projects as long as their schedule allows three inspections of the owner's project per week and regular consultations by phone and in person.

(See part 2 of "Owner Controlled Contracting", construction Advisor job description, responsibilities, and suggested compensation")

Continue Personal selections for Price

(See Items Requiring Owner Selection checklist Tab 5)
(See Owner Selections Deadlines Tab 5)

At this point, your personal selections should begin to form decorating themes for various rooms and involve matching colors and textures. The most complex mix of selections occurs in the kitchen but other rooms also need style selections. Carry floor and carpet samples, Formica chips, and color samples with you in a very large brief case to make comparisons.

Use the personal selections checklist in references as a guide, keep accurate and organized records. You will need them to make final selections, to place orders on time and have materials available for installation when needed. Subcontractors also need to know what installation preparations are required and what needs to fit where. This is especially true for appliances, plumbing fixtures, and lighting fixtures.

If you carry a copy of the preliminary plans with you <u>Do Not</u> give them out or make copies. A preliminary layout can find its way into the hands of a supplier or installer before final working drawings are finished. Many problems and delays are the result of using incomplete drawings.

If you choose to work with an interior designer, <u>restrict their advice and assistance to colors and textures.</u> If they begin to suggest changes in room arrangements, window locations etc. inform them that any physical design change suggestions must be made directly to your Home Designer/Architect. The best way to create doubt and confusion is to engage an outside design source that offers alternate design ideas while working drawings are in progress.

Continue Searching for Subcontractors and Construction Material Suppliers

(See subcontractors and suppliers needed checklists Tab 5)

In less than one month, you will approve the final working drawings and begin to solicit bids and prices. Your list of potential subcontractors and suppliers should be nearly complete with enough options to assemble a good team. Consult with your Construction Advisor for opinions and suggestions for any missing essential players. Call selected subcontractors and suppliers to see if they are still available and interested, let them know you will be using a an experienced builder/contractor as a Construction Advisor but "you" will still have primary responsibility for scheduling and payments. Let them know that working drawings will be available in a few weeks for bids. <u>Steel or manufactured wood beams and support posts, if specified, will be one of the first deliveries needed. Locate this supplier early.</u>

NOTE: Avoid square foot pricing. Square foot pricing is a guess based upon the false premise that the simple act of multiplying a floor size by an assumed dollar amount will produce an accurate forecast cost. Square foot pricing has value only in producing the roughest of estimates. If all you want is a dollar amount within +/- 30%, use square foot pricing. If your budget or loan limit requires you to be more accurate, there is only one way to arrive at a reliable forecast cost and that is to price all the pieces and parts, all the labor and materials, and add them together. You would never by a car by the pound and should never price a house by the square foot. The bid addendum letter in Tab 6 asks for man-hour and material prices prompts subcontractors to avoid square foot estimates.

DESIGN and PLANNING CALENDAR

MONTHS FOUR and FIVE

Approve the final design
Select subcontractors and material suppliers
Solicit labor and material bids
Arrive at an accurate forecast cost
Secure financing
Contract with selected sub trades and suppliers
Obtain permits

NOTE: Do not clear, work on, or park, anything on your building site without a building permit and the bank's approval

Approve the Final Design

(See Reading Blueprints Tab 2)

Evaluating and Approving the Working Drawings

Working drawings differ from preliminary drawings in their completeness and detail. They also differ in their intent. Preliminary drawings communicate to the owners what their new home will look like and how it will function. Floor plans have few dimensions and avoid details to make it easy for owners to visualize furniture placements and traffic patterns. Exterior views on preliminary drawings are also kept clear of details owner's don't need. Unnecessary information on preliminary drawings are a distraction preventing owners from properly evaluating their future home.

Working drawings have a different purpose and a different audience. Working drawings include all of the information contained in the preliminary drawings, but add all the instructions, details, and information needed by approving bodies and those providing materials and labor to build the home. Working drawings are cluttered with dimensions and details needed by building inspectors, suppliers, and tradesmen.

Have your designer or a heating contractor complete the required heat loss calculations for your house and fill out the REScheck forms needed for a building permit. Make any changes needed for compliance before distributing drawings for bids. This is the last opportunity to spot errors or make voluntary changes. After working drawings are distributed, there will be a large number of drawings in circulation. Changing all of them will be impossible and any unchanged plans can cause erroneous bids and construction errors.

You are generally not capable of evaluating every detail in working drawings but should review the final working drawings with your designer and your Construction Advisor. When you are satisfied with the drawings, sign a copy and submit them for permits.

NOTE: Eliminate any square footage annotations on the working drawings before releasing them for bidding. If square footage is required for permits, add them only to drawings submitted to the approval agencies. Square foot bidding is discouraged. Detailed pricing is preferred.

Solicit Labor and Material Bids

(Use Bid Request Forms, Tab 6)

There are two major cost components common to any construction project, (Labor and Materials). Arriving at an accurate forecast cost for your project requires an understanding of how the many individual labor and material price components are determined, what they are composed of, and how to check them for accuracy. It is impossible, in a single-family custom home project, to forecast a final cost with precision. It is possible, however, to limit pricing errors and arrive at an acceptable estimate. It is easy to check material prices and add reasonable handling charges. It is not easy to check labor bids and add reasonable overhead costs. It is even more difficult to check combined labor and material bids. To complicate the custom home bidding / pricing process further, many talented residential tradesmen are unable to use sophisticated cost forecasting methods. The result is reasonable guesses based on experience and the use of square feet to quantify their guess.

To assist the owner in evaluating labor-only bids, addendum requests for simple man-hour estimates are included in "Forms in the reference section". The addendums should accompany requests for both "labor only" and "labor and material" bids. The requests are not intimidating, ask for estimates only, and are not mandatory. Addendum information submitted with bids will assist you in scheduling and in evaluating the accuracy of bids.

Evaluating material prices requires effort and the ability to use the blueprints to determine material quantities. A guide to estimating material quantities, and where to find prices, is included in "Reading Blueprints in references".

To distribute blueprints for bidding, scan the complete set of approved final drawings onto a thumb drive and make four printed copies for yourself. (Printing and mailing many sets of drawings for bidding can be expensive and time consuming). Some bidders will have access to blueprint machines, but for those that don't, FedEx Kinko's, Staples and other printing companies have services allowing you to email the drawings as an attachment for printout on demand. Kinko's and Staples are especially useful because they use a service that holds submissions for twenty-four hours and allows multiple retrievals and printouts at any of their US stores. E-mail submissions to the services are free. The service will send the submitter, (you), a retrieval number that you can forwarded to bidders. Using the retrieval number your suppliers and subcontractors can pay for and retrieve the drawings during a twenty-four hour pickup period at any US store.

Send scanned blueprints to printandgo@kinkos.com or staples@printme.com and they will send you a pick up number with instructions. Forward the number and instructions to all your bidders. Repeat the free process as many times as needed.

Back up your scanned blueprints in your computer.

Select bidders from the lists of potential subcontractors and suppliers collected over the last three months. Contact them to see if they are still interested and if their schedule will accommodate a project starting in about .... weeks. If they are interested, confirm their mailing and email addresses, tell them you are soliciting several bids and will send them an addendum but will accept their usual format. (Confirming their mailing address is an important check on their legitimacy). Tell them you will e-mail the house plans to Staples or FedEx Kinko's, and provide them with a pickup number for printing. Bidders pay for printing at pick-up. Include the bidding information request appropriate to the type of bid.

Bidding for a residential construction project can take several forms; *labor and materials, materials only, and labor only*. To control costs and limit overbidding, ask *labor and material* bidders to specify the cost of materials and estimated man hours needed to assemble the materials. Unfortunately, this separation of labor and materials is not common in residential bidding. Most do not use sophisticated methods and make educated guesses based on experience. The "Bid information request forms" in the appendix encourage detailed bidding but some bidders will not be capable of responding accurately. Use caution. Insisting on detailed bidding may discourage very capable subcontractors.

As you and your Construction Advisor review bids, look for unreasonably low bids as well as unreasonably high bids. One way for a subcontractor to inform the owners that they do not want the job is to, intentionally overbid. In contrast, a competent subcontractor interested in the work but with poor pricing skills may underbid. If this contractor is preferred, contact them to be certain they understand the scope of work involved and give them a chance to adjust their bid upward. Ask all bidders to provide all fasteners, (nails, screws, glue, etc.), and to include their cost in their bids

It is sometimes advantageous to have a larger company bid electrical, plumbing and heating as a package. Having the mechanical aspects of the project under one umbrella simplifies scheduling and avoids construction site conflicts. It is also advantages to add certain minor tasks to framing labor bids like asking the framing crew to apply felt to the roof as they apply the roof sheathing to provide a temporary rain cover until the roofing crew can arrive.

To spot and control overbidding, it is often advantages to develop or solicit your own material lists for job segments that are bid as *labor and materials*. Examples are roofing, insulation, drywall, and occasionally framing.

Select subcontractors and material suppliers

With your Construction Advisor's advice, choose which subcontractors and material suppliers you want to build your new home. Contact your choices to be certain they are still available and insure that nothing has changed in the plans or their bid. Give them an approximate date for the start of work and arrange for any formal agreements needed.

Contract with Selected Subcontractors and Suppliers

Residential Subcontractors often contract with known General Contractors using informal handshakes and verbal agreements. Others use a combination of a bid form / agreement to consummate a contract for work. A detailed legal agreement may be offered by larger firms and intimidate small contracting individuals. Use your best judgment. Formal legal agreements can sometimes create more problems than they solve. A simple agreement to complete the work in a professional and timely manner, to meet building codes, to notify the owner if an unavoidable delay occurs, and to respond to calls from the owner and the Construction Advisor, is usually sufficient. Keep your bidding files current. A back-up sub contractor could be needed.

Arrive at an Accurate Forecast Cost.

The only way to arrive at an accurate forecast cost for a custom home is to individually price as many elements of the home as possible and carefully estimate those that cannot. Checklists provide a partial list of major elements but there are other costs including,

Administration and supervision
Insurance
Financing charges
Delays and overrun estimates
Miscellaneous unexpected

Owner selections of decorator items come with individual prices. Quotes for construction materials by lumber companies, however, rarely disclose individual prices or quantity breakdowns. Computing detailed construction material lists requires an investment of company time and the detailed lists are protected as proprietary. This makes it difficult for you to compare or evaluate the pricing of a large segment of your construction costs.

The best way to overcome this obstacle is to specify truckloads that reflect stages of framing, and have the loads priced individually. (if possible)

- Load 1 First floor deck framing materials / beams
- Load 2 First floor walls framing materials
- Load 3 Second floor deck framing materials
- Load 4 Second floor walls framing materials
- Load 5 Roof framing / trusses / sheathing materials
- Load 6 Roof covering materials, flashing / drip edge / ice guard / vents / felt / shingles / other
- Load 7 Windows / sliding glass doors

Having the total construction materials broken down into loads has several advantages. It allows deliveries to be coordinated with construction progress, allows combined loads if needed, to stay ahead of the framers, and breaks the total construction material package down into small parts easier to price for comparison. Manufactured beams, trusses and Loads 6 & 7 may be available from separate sources at reduced prices.

NOTE: Window sizes must match the opening sizes and wall thicknesses specified on working drawings

If you have the time, you can approximate the lumber companies list by using the instructions in References to calculate construction material quantities and then look up Big Box on-line prices. The effort to calculate and price construction materials in advance, using your working drawings, can help determine feasibility and can also help determine if the bid is reasonable. Most owners avoid this time consuming exercise but it can pinpoint overbids and save money.

Secure Financing

Having adequate construction funds available is essential. Running short of funds near the end of a construction project can be disastrous. Lending institutions make every effort to limit their liabilities and shy away from poorly planned projects, especially owner managed projects. Some lenders require a general contractor as an additional construction loan signatory. This requirement is not compatible with a Construction Advisor arrangement, which does not require them to have bonding or liability insurance. Some banks also attempt to limit their liability by requiring plans to be completed and stamped by a registered architect, usually specifying a particular architect. This arrangement is not compatible with designs done by the owner or designs by an experienced home designer. Most State laws and nearly all building departments, however, allow designs by individuals other than architects. The trend in residential construction financing is to finance more owner-managed projects when they are well planned.

Often missed by experts and lenders, is how the structure of a construction loan can negatively affect the ability of an owner or contractor to make timely payments to subcontractors and suppliers. Some construction loans put residential construction projects in jeopardy by requiring a large deposit to secure the loan and then delay disbursements until a significant part of the project is completed. Delays in disbursements of funds to cover costs force the owner, or general contractor, to make large additional out of pocket payments to avoid mechanics liens.

This deficit condition can occur when loan conditions limit disbursement to the completion of major phases. An example is withholding a first disbursement until the foundation is complete and has been inspected by the local building department, and then again by the banking inspector. With each inspection taking up to two-weeks, and with deposits and payments for supplies due in advance before the foundation is complete creates a serious deficit. Payments due before the lending institution will disburse funds are common in this type of arrangement and put the project in a late payment status from the beginning.

Starting in an arrears position can continue throughout the project creating delays, liens, and problems.

Owners should carefully examine the requirements for the disbursement of funds and balance potential delays against other advantages the loan may offer. Discuss disbursement policies with the lending officer and use the Construction Calendar along with the detailed pricing developed by quotes, bids and selections to forecast when payments will become due. A loan agreement that disburses funds upon the presentation of a legitimate invoice works much better than disbursements based on stages of completion.

Obtain Permits

With working drawings approved by the owner, the permitting process can begin. The first approval needed is often by an architectural review board to be certain the proposed home meets local deed restrictions. The next permit is often a zoning permit to determine if the proposed home is in a permitted zone and meets the requirements of homes in the proposed building area. Other permits may be required if utilities need to be extended, if curb cuts are required, if there are unusual soil conditions, if the building site is in a flood plain, or if a well or septic system is required. The final permit is nearly always the building permit. If there is any doubt as to prerequisite approvals needed for a building permit, inquire at the building department. The entire permitting process should take only a few weeks but can take several months. Being prepared with requisite data, site plans, and complete house plans will avoid delays. Continue to make final personal selections during permitting delays. Meetings with your Construction Advisor should also take place and selected sub contractors and suppliers should be notified that a building permit will be issued soon.

PLANNING/DESIGN AND PRICING

PART 2
PRICING GUIDES

The following guides will help you accomplish the planning and pricing steps listed in the planning calendar. The calendars tell you what you should be working on. The guides give you additional advice as how to accomplish the tasks listed. The guides are not detail specific. Custom home projects vary widely but all share common sequencing and management challenges. Use the guides to keep the process in perspective and to set priorities.

PRICING GUIDES

Locating Sub Contractors

Locating Construction Material Suppliers

Soliciting and Evaluating Labor Bids

Soliciting and Evaluating Construction Material Bids

Soliciting and Evaluating Combined Labor / Material Bids

Selecting, Pricing, and Ordering, Personal Selections

Contracting with Sub Contractors & Suppliers

Guide to Locating Subcontractors

(See subcontractors needed checklist Tab 5, page)
(See phone scripts Tab 3, page)

It is important to get a complete set of all of the labor bids needed to arrive at an accurate forecast cost for your project. It is also important to set priorities for making final choices for awarding contracts by contracting those you will need first as early as possible. Your files become especially important here, as does your judgment. The lowest bid is not necessarily the best selection. Many other factors will influence your decision as to which bid to include in your final cost and which sub contractor to use. It is important to get as many bids as possible for several reasons. Being able to compare several similar bids often highlights an egregious bidding error by a contractor you are giving serious consideration. Having several potential sub contractors capable of doing the same work, gives you a back up. There are four parts to a final forecast cost; (1) labor bids, (2) estimates by suppliers, (3) owner selection prices, and (4), expenses, including financing costs.

Organizations like Angie's List and Home Advisor have opened the door for owners to manage their own custom home project by making essential labor skills available without relying on the builder buddy system. Home Advisor and Angie's List referrals also provide the assurance of a background check.

To search beyond Home Advisor and Angie's list, ask lumber companies, use the phone book, check with local building departments and get referrals from friends, and prospective Construction Advisors. Smaller contracting firms are usually more adaptable and better suited to residential single home projects, but don't overlook larger companies, especially if they combine electrical heating and plumbing services.

Beyond expertise and experience, stability is the most important attribute to look for in essential sub contractors, especially those that will be involved in more than one phase of the project. A roofing contractor, for example, completes the application of materials and is called back only for repairs or oversights. An electrician, on the other hand, can be involved in various phases of the project from start to finish. Replacing a contractor with multi-phase responsibilities in mid-phase, requires the replacement subcontractor to accept or re-do previous work, assume responsibility for the finished product, and possibly obtain and pay for a new permit.

Financial stability in subcontractors is also important. All subcontractors require expensive tools, reliable transportation, and either reasonable credit or enough cash to provide transportation, stockpile mortar, fasteners, glue, compressors, scaffolding etc. Subcontractors also expect regular and prompt payments for work completed. Most residential subcontractors will be Mom-and-Pop companies with few employees. A credit check and a check on the subcontractor's reliability is advisable, especially for multi-phase subcontractors. A back up prospect for each essential contractor is also advisable. Things as simple as a family illness can put their efforts and your project on hold.

When you call a prospective subcontractor, ask if they would be interested in giving you a quote as soon as the final drawings are ready. Tell them you will be managing the project but will have a Construction Advisor helping you. Briefly describe his duties, (see chapter four). Ask what services the subcontractor provides and what materials they provide. When they ask about the project all you can provide, In advance of the working-drawings, is a general description, like, a medium sized two-story colonial, an estimated start date, and a location. Do not give out square footage or preliminary drawings. What you want is a show of interest, some free advice, and a contact you can call with questions when you begin soliciting quotes. If you give out details before they are final, Subcontractors may use over-simplified pricing methods and plug in a price determined by what they need rather than a realistic cost plus bid.

You are looking for recent new home construction experience and a few references. Many of the tradesmen you will contact will operate out of their homes and may be difficult to contact. Don't give up. Being too busy to answer their home/office phone during working hours may be a good sign. It may also be a sign that they are hiding from creditors or other work obligations. Ask about the difficulty in contacting them, and if they use a cell phone on the job. Ask what jobs they are working on now, when they expect to complete current obligations, and if the current job is demanding all of their time. Explain that on your job, a refusal to answer or return phone calls promptly won't be acceptable but reasonable delays are expected.

The time you spend contacting as many potential subcontractors as possible is not a waste of time. What you learn and whom you meet during this relaxed investigative phase allows you to visualize the types of labor you will need.

Skip this phase and you will have to learn as you go during construction and may have to repeat the process if you need a back-up subcontractor. Contact and make phone friends with as many local tradesmen as possible, but remember; construction trades have similar interest and problems and talk to each other often. Be discrete, polite, and never critical of a competitor's work or reputation. Keep accurate records of your contacts and later, when you are ready for bids, you will be calling acquaintances instead of strangers.

Use the scripted calling guides (TAB 3) to locate and become acquainted with potential subcontractors prior to soliciting bids.

Guide to Locating Construction Material Suppliers

(See Construction Material Suppliers needed checklist Tab 5, page 203)
(See scripted calling guides Tab 3, page 133)

Construction Material suppliers, (lumber, concrete, windows, roof trusses, etc.), are different from suppliers of owner-selected items, (toilets, cabinets, doorknobs, floor coverings, etc.). Being aware of the various construction materials needed is important, keeping track of their costs is essential. Locating and evaluating potential construction material suppliers is easier than locating and evaluating subcontractors. There are normally only a few building supply companies servicing a local area and they are usually large companies with public tax and operating records. Ask your Construction Advisor for their opinion of local lumber and material suppliers. The phone numbers of local lumber and supply companies are readily available. Call and tell them you will have the final working drawings for a new custom home in the next few weeks and will need to have lumber, trusses, roofing materials, windows and doors, priced and reviewed by your Construction Advisor and the construction lender. Try to arrange a meeting with a salesperson, preferably at their primary business location. The lumber/materials supplier you select will become an essential partner during construction. Your contact at this supplier can work with you to keep your project on schedule or cause costly delays. It is essential that your relationship with your major materials supplier be open and respectful. Make certain you are comfortable and have a good working relationship with this key part of your project. You will be calling to ask for lead times, to schedule deliveries, and to as for advice often. Make this business relationship as personal as possible, first names etc.

A secretary will answer your initial call to a construction supplier and will put you in contact with a salesperson who is accustomed to all kinds of inquiries. For this reason, scripted calling guides are unnecessary when calling construction material suppliers.

Some construction material suppliers handle a limited number of window and door brands. Check materials specified in your house plans with the supplier for availability. Substitutions may conflict with your plan's specifications and cause framing errors.

Other construction materials, (like gravel and concrete), can often be supplied through a subcontractor but some require an owner selection, (like siding type and color). Some construction materials may also require the owner to pay for them directly, (like owner-selected special roofing materials). These special cases and similar ones are easily resolved when they occur.

As confusing as all this sounds, who supplies what and who pays for what falls into place quickly during the bidding phase.

DESIGNING/PLANNING AND PRICING

During the pricing phase, the owner should make it clear to construction material suppliers that they, the owner, will be purchasing and paying for the materials. Some suppliers will not quote prices directly to owners to avoid expensive pricing efforts for individuals who are curious but not serious. A completed set of professional house plans with the owner's name on them is sometimes enough to convince a supplier that a major pricing effort is worth their time. When blueprints are not enough, have your Construction Advisor intervene, but have him be careful not to create any personal obligations.

Having individual material prices for as many components of your new home as possible allows you to evaluate material prices, when bid as a package, and some labor prices, when bid as labor and materials.

For example; a concrete contractor submits a $10,000 labor-and-material bid to pour your driveway and tells you he will use a four-man crew and will complete the job in only one day. With help, you calculate the cubic yards of concrete, and the cost of gravel for a 4" gravel base and throw in $200 for forming materials, $500 for overhead, $400 for equipment, a generous $2,000 profit, and $30/hour for four men for ten hours. You arrive at a total of $6,000, half the bid price. This tells you the contractor is planning on a profit of $6, 000 for one days work.

Knowing the actual cost of materials and estimating profits, overhead and labor costs can avoid both over-bids and under-bids, and signal a need to negotiate a reasonable price, or seek other bids. Reasonable costs and profits are expected. Bids based on guestimates can be dangerous. Bids intended to take advantage of an inexperienced owner are not acceptable. When a bid is questionable, check your addition, ask for an explanation, and either help them arrive at a realistic price or seek another contractor. A Construction Advisor's experience can be of help, but they may also be unwilling or incapable of calculating material quantities. The calculations take time and when other simpler material package comparisons are available they are usually left up to material suppliers.

For obsessive-compulsive owners, formula for calculating various construction material quantities are available in chapter 10.

Big Box Retailers, like Lowes, Canards, or Home Depot provide on-line per piece prices you can use to calculate approximate total costs for many of the materials you will need. Keep in mind that home improvement retailers "staff and stock" to service occasional one-time buyers and small projects, not whole house projects. Retail stores focus on rotating popular "on the shelf items" as quickly as possible from the back of the store, through the cash register, and out the front door, and are generally not prepared for large loads that needs to be stored outside until needed by the customer.

Departments, like floor coverings, kitchens, and appliances, supplement retail sales efforts and are subject to the same "push to sell" and "move merchandise quickly" emphasis. Installations provided by retail chains are through local tradesmen, contracted by the store, and can come with a higher rate of mistakes and delays. Working with Big Box Retailers is convenient and may save a few dollars but you should balance their offerings against the advantages of firms more focused on larger projects.

<u>Examine Potential Lumber Suppliers</u>
Lumber is definitely better if purchased from an established larger lumber company. Some of these have become retail chains following the example of the Big Boxes but others have remained independent. Talk to both and ask if they offer lumber take-off services, (using blueprints to calculate a complete lumber list). Ask about roof trusses and laminated beams. Meet with lumber sales at their place of business if possible. Big Box Retailers may offer take-off services and large shipments but they are not good at it, especially for whole house packages.

Guide to Soliciting and Evaluating Labor Bids

If you were diligent in locating potential sub contractors during the planning phase, you have a list of bidders waiting on working drawings and ready to bid. Using the names in your files and the sub contractors needed checklist in Tab 5, call sub contractors you find suitable. Arrange to send them a set of approved drawings and email them a bid request. (See Forms Tab 6)

The best way to distribute drawings is to use an on-line printing service. Have Fedex-Kinko's, Staples, or any blueprint service scan the blueprints to a thumb drive, then use your laptop to email the drawings to printme@staples.com or printandgo@fedex.com. Printme or Printandgo will send you a retrieval number. Forward the number to all potential bidders along with the appropriate bid form. Sub contractors can then, (within 24 hours), go to any Staples or Kinko's near them with the retrieval code, and pay for and receive a complete set of drawings.

Keep in mind that bids from mom-and-pop operations are often not based on sophisticated pricing methods. They are often, based on square foot estimates or guesses based on experience. Bids may also contain a hidden message like, "I don't really want this job but, at a grossly inflated price, I'll take it", or, "I'm desperate and have bid below what is reasonable because I need the money". Use the bid request forms provided to try to get additional information from bidders. Asking bidders to think through their bids in more detail will hopefully, improve their accuracy. Having more details included in bids will also allow you to arrive at your own estimates and make comparisons. Your Construction Advisor may also be accustomed to making guestimate bids but their experience can still be of great help in evaluating bids and bidders and in making final decisions.

It is important to get a complete set of all of the labor bids needed to arrive at an accurate forecast cost for your project. It is also important to set priorities for making final choices for awarding contracts by contracting those you will need first as early as possible. Your files become especially important here, as does your judgment. The lowest bid is not necessarily the best selection. Many other factors will influence your decision as to which sub contractor to use. It is important to get as many bids as possible for several reasons. Being able to compare several similar bids often highlights an egregious bidding error by a contractor you are giving serious consideration. Having several potential sub contractors capable of doing the same work, gives you a back up.

Refer to your *project files* for subcontractors you have decided are good prospects. Refer to the *subcontractors needed checklist* to be certain you have a complete list of the subcontractors you need to solicit for bids. Call prospective bidders to determine their continued interest and availability. With the help of your Construction Advisor, follow up on bid submissions and. continue to press for bids until you have at least two reasonable proposals for each labor segment needed.

Consultations may be required to arrive at an acceptable proposal from a preferred tradesmen lacking in the cost-forecasting skills needed to create an accurate bid. This problem is common in residential construction, even among builders and general contractors, and is part of the reason repetitive designs and projects are preferred. It is also why an owner, with organizational and management skills, can smooth out, and reduce costs in custom home projects through active participation. If a preferred bidder hesitates because of a fear of over or under bidding and, if help is warranted, finding someone qualified to assist them may be a good idea.

Some subcontractor services are required soon after the construction begins others are not needed until near the end. Concentrate on securing early labor needs first. Review the construction calendar to set priorities. The inability to secure an excavator or a framing crew will delay or stop your project before it gets started. Not having a trim carpenter's bid leaves a hole in your pricing, but won't become critical for months.

Bidding In residential construction is more one of qualification than competition and the lowest bid may not be the best bid. Select and contract, either formally or by a handshake, with the labor only contractors that will be available when you need them, appear reliable, are experienced, are familiar with the materials they will apply or assemble, and will provide the labor required at a reasonable price.

Labor only contractors need to supply, except for specialty clips and supports, any nails, screws and common fasteners they will need. Owner supplied items include. Plate straps, hurricane clips, joist supports, beam mounts, subfloor glue, etc. To be certain assembly materials required are not overlooked a review of each labor bid type is advisable.

Bidding to determine a total cost for the project is important. Bidding also helps to eliminate over or under bids. Soliciting prices for services and materials is also a way to make the bidding process a friendly conversation, not a contest. If negotiations are necessary, make them a friendly discussion of alternative ways to arrive at a forecast cost.

Guide to Soliciting and Evaluating Construction Material Bids

(See construction-material-suppliers needed Tab 5, page 203)
(Use scripted calling guides Tab 3, page 133)

Like the food you buy, residential construction materials, arrive at their final destination after a long chain of harvesting, manufacturing, wholesale distributions, and retail outlets.

Buying from a large lumber company is like shopping at Sam's Club where bulk sales result in a discount. Buying from a home improvement store is like shopping at your local grocery store, paying full price and expecting fewer services. Knowing where to shop for bulk is important in both groceries and construction materials. If you are buying food for your family, a neighborhood grocery store is convenient and sufficient. If you are buying for a restaurant, Sam's Club is the better option. The same logic applies to purchasing construction materials. For a small project, a home improvement store is appropriate, but for a whole-house project, a lumber company is a better choice.

Most lumber companies have their own printing services allowing you to provide them with a set of working drawings by inserting your designated blueprint thumb drive into your laptop and sending the drawings via e-mail. Lumber companies also have the advantage of an assigned lumber salesperson, a point of contact that can help you with, "brand and type", staging deliveries, and in understanding price breakdowns. With your salesperson, review what you want priced, (use the construction materials checklist), what materials you would like quoted separately, (so you can compare them to other sources), and the brands of doors, windows, roofing materials, and manufactured structural components they carry. Involve your Construction Advisor when necessary. Another consideration when deciding where to obtain construction material pricing is return policies. Being able to return damaged or unused materials can result in considerable savings. Large lumber companies are more accommodating when construction materials are involved and may pick up returns.

Your blueprints provide the information needed to calculate the construction materials needed to construct the basement, floors, walls, the roof, etc. The blueprints specify the type and size of most items but a few selections may be necessary. Your salesperson may ask you to choose things like, window color, door design, interior wood trim profiles, etc.

Comparing construction material quotes by price alone can be difficult. Quotes may be in board feet instead of price per piece, and may be in different formats. Comparing material bids often comes down to more than final price comparisons. The most important evaluation of bids you can make is to determine if the bid is reasonable.

Keep your construction material prices separate from your personally selected item prices.

For owners willing to make the additional effort and with extra time available, guides for calculating construction materials are included in Tab 7

Guide to Soliciting and Evaluating Combined Labor / Material Bids

Combined labor and material bids, compound the difficulty of assessing or comparing bids. A first consideration in evaluating combined labor/material bids is to determine if the bid is reasonable. The only way to do this is to break the bid down into its key components. The two major components are, of course, labor and materials, and there are several ways to separate them. The most direct is to ask bidders to separate labor and material charges. Very few will be willing to do this, not because they are hiding something, but because they don't calculate residential bids using complex formulas using, material costs, man-hours, overhead, and profit. A full formula effort is not worth the bidder's time in residential projects. To arrive at a bid for a residential job, bidders often compare square footage or other gross measurements to past residential jobs to determine if their offering is reasonable. For you to determine if the bid is reasonable however, you need to separate labor charges from material charges.

To break out the labor portion of a labor/material bid you need man-hour estimates, but most residential contractors don't use and don't have this information. To avoid asking for something bidders don't have, or won't share, ask a less demanding question, (see bid request forms). Instead of asking for a labor and material breakdown or estimated man-hours, ask bidders to estimate how long it will take to complete their portion of the project. Knowing the time the job will take, not only helps you schedule work and deliveries, it also gives you a rough way to estimate man-hours.

To estimate man-hours, guess, or ask, how many tradesmen will be working on the job. From the number of workers, and the number of days they will work, you can estimate man-hours, multiply estimated man-hours by an estimated per hour cost, (include, pay rates, matching SS, benefits, etc), Add estimated equipment costs for trucks and tools, estimated overhead expenses, insurance, bonding and estimated profits. You now have a very rough estimate for the labor portion of the bid.

To estimate the material portion of a labor and material bid, calculate the materials needed using the take-off formulas in Tab 7 and look up individual prices on-line. Begin by using the blueprints to determine key take-off measurements, (square footage of the first and second floors, the linier footage of first and second floor outside walls, the linier footage of interior walls on both floors, and the square footage of the roof). Using these key measurements and the basic formulae in Tab 7 makes calculating construction material quantities easy.

Prices for construction materials are available on home-improvement store web sites. Prices from store web sites will differ from prices available to most subcontractors but we are after a rough estimate not a definitive price. Multiply estimated quantities by on-line prices, and add taxes and estimated handling costs to arrive at rough total material costs. Add estimated labor costs to obtain an estimated labor and material amount. Compare your estimates to labor/material bids to determine if they are reasonable.

Keep in mind that these calculated man-hour and material-costs are rough estimates and won't determine a best price, they will however, be close enough to determine if a combined labor and material bid is reasonable.

This may seem complicated but it is just multiplying "How Many" *times* "How Long" *times* "Dollars" to get labor costs and "How Much" *times* "Dollars" to get material costs, and adding them together. To get ahead of estimating chores, use your architects scale and your blueprints to determine and record the key take-off measurements listed in chapter 10 and make them a part of your permanent files. Key take-off measurements simplify estimating efforts and allow construction material amounts to be determined easily.

Guide to Locating, Pricing, and Ordering, Personal Selections

Construction materials like lumber and drywall need some basic oversight to insure quality but, except for items like window brands and basement types determined during the design process, construction materials do not require the owner to express a preference.

Items such as lighting fixtures, bathtubs and floor coverings however, require owners to express their preference, select specific items, and coordinate selected items for fit, color, texture etc. Owner selections are a large and very important part of custom home planning, pricing and construction and are required of owners regardless of their degree of involvement in construction management.

In *standard-model* home building, owner preferences are limited by restricting choices to a few offerings displayed in the garages of model homes. By making decorator selections a part of the sales contract, the price of a new home is predetermined and the customer/builder interface is simplified.

In *builder-controlled* custom home projects, a total cost is required before construction begins. To establish a final contract cost, the cost of owner-selected items is included in construction contracts as allowances, (specified maximum amounts the owner can spend on selection items before additional funding is required).

In *owner-controlled* custom home projects, (as described in this guide), owners must price preliminary selections early to establish a forecast cost and later, to meet construction deadlines, make final selections with shipping and manufacturing delays in mind. A selections checklist is included in chapter 9 to help you meet these deadlines.

Starting with choosing a building site and ending with landscaping details, personal selections continue throughout the custom home design/build process. Keeping track of options and prices will fill much of your project files and involve much of your time. Think of the selection process as a once in a lifetime shopping spree. Diligence in making preliminary selections "for price", and in keeping accurate records, will make final selections easy. Having short lists of items to select from, prices to compare, contacts available, lead times established, and details predetermined, narrows final choices and makes ordering simple. You can begin making preliminary selections even before design work begins. Start early.

To keep the selection process in perspective, think first of the outside of your new home and what decorator choices you need to make. These choices will come up during the design phase and include siding, stone or brick, and roof type and color. Start early by collecting catalogs, looking on-line, touring neighborhoods with a camera, and by visiting supplier showrooms.

Next, think inside your home beginning with the interior background style that special ceilings, interior trim, stair types, railings, and interior door styles will establish. Again, collect catalogs, look on-line and visit showrooms.

Next, think room-by-room. Begin with rooms that have plumbing fixtures. Make preliminary plumbing fixture selections early, they may affect the design layout. Keep accurate records, (where you found it, what you selected, where it goes in the house, price, details, and contacts).

Next, think cabinetry. Begin with the utility room and bathrooms. Save the kitchen and major built-ins for last and make your initial selections truly preliminary. Establishing accurate preliminary prices may involve kitchen designer requests for preliminary drawings that cannot be released. Per-foot prices for cabinetry and countertops will suffice as a preliminary estimate.

Next, Think floor types and floor coverings room-by-room. Start with tile and wood floors, leaving carpeting for last. Wood and tile is priced by the square foot. Carpeting is priced by the square yard. Measure rooms on your blueprints to get rough square footages for preliminary pricing. Pad your measurements for waste.

Finally, think appliances and lighting fixtures. Try to get these priced as "installed". An independent lighting fixture showroom will usually include a knowledgeable salesperson and offer installation services. Home improvement stores offer choices for less important and less expensive lighting choices.

Examine Potential Plumbing Suppliers

Plumbing fixtures including tubs and showers are essential items specified on your house plans and require an owner selection. Ask about availability, and lead times. Try for a color chip you can carry around to coordinate with other selections. Faucets, molded vanity tops, even flush handles may require a selection. Be conservative. An off-white toilet is much easier to decorate around than a red one

Examine Potential Electrical/ Lighting Fixture suppliers

You will choose the color of your electrical plates, and the type of light switches etc. Your electrical sub contractor is the best final source for these items but having reviewed them in advance will save time and confusion, especially if you have a sample available. Choose lighting fixtures with the help of a professional and supplied by a large lighting fixture store. It is also to your advantage if the store provides installation. Electricians are reluctant to install expensive fixtures.

Examine Potential Appliance Suppliers

Big Box Retailers will have the largest variety of brands. Smaller appliance stores may specialize in brands but shouldn't be overlooked. Like larger plumbing items, appliances are must have and must fit items that also require a decorating approach. Start coordinating your kitchen early.

Other Selections

You will be using this list later to make final selections but having located needed suppliers in advance and having a name to call will save time and make coordinating the construction phase much easier. Some selections are made through the installer/ contractor. Others you will need to make available to the appropriate sub contractor or make your choice known for him to purchase and provide.

(See Items requiring owner selection checklist in Tab 5, page 205)
(See deadlines for selections in Tab 5, page 213)

Keeping accurate records of shopping excursions for preliminary prices is extremely important. Making reasonable choices to arrive at an accurate total forecast cost requires owners to recall and compare the results of many trips to showrooms and stores, the results of many on line searches, and the results of many catalog inquiries. An organized history of searches and results makes comparisons easy and becomes a valuable guide to making final selections.

Stay organized by using the checklists provided and by arranging your files and searches according to the six primary search categories.

- Exterior selections
- Interior style selections, trim doors etc.
- Plumbing fixtures
- Cabinetry and counter tops
- Flooring
- Appliances and lighting fixtures

Guide to Contracting with Sub Contractors & Suppliers

A contract is an enforceable agreement stating the responsibilities and obligations of the parties involved. It can be twenty pages of responsibilities and obligations followed by twenty more pages of enforcement methods and penalties. It can also be a handshake. Residential construction contracts are usually much closer to a handshake than a 40-page document. One reason is that damage from default or unintentional errors is usually a small part of the total cost of the project. Another is that fixing an oversight or replacing a subcontractor is easier and has less impact on cost and completion than involving lawyers. When a disagreement arises, it is often wiser to make a final payment, tear up the contract and move on. Suing for damages is a long process involving the owner, subcontractors, suppliers, inspectors, approving agencies and more. This may present an appealing opportunity for lawyers but will taint and possibly stall an entire project.

Detailed construction contracts are available on line or can be prepared specifically for your project, but most small residential contractors will shy away from excessive and difficult to understand requirements and preconditions. An agreement stating the scope of work, materials needed, quality expected, a price and terms of payment, and an estimated time for completion, all stated in simple terms, is more common in residential construction than lengthy documentary preparations for court.

The first document available as a potential contract is the subcontractor's or material suppliers quote or bid. If it is acceptable, use it as the contract, if some parts are questionable or seem to hold the bidder harmless for mistakes or oversights that you think should be their responsibility, have it reviewed and suggest revisions. For subcontracted work, try to obtain an estimate of how long the work will take. Reputation and references provide a better assurance of quality work than a written contract. With sufficient oversight and prompt payments there should be few problems.

CONSTRUCTION

PART 1
CONSTRUCTION MANAGEMENT

If you have completed the "design, planning, and pricing phase", you have completed the difficult half of the project. If you have established a working relationship with your construction advisor, selected sub contractors, have approved the final design, met deed restrictions, and obtained a building permit, you are ready, with your financial institutions approval, (don't do anything without their final approval), to notified utilities, clear the building site, and have the house staked out for excavation.

CONSTRUCTION CALENDAR

Seven-Month Construction Calendar

Three Months to Dry and Secure

Lot clearing and excavation	2 weeks
Foundation / organizing the building site	3 weeks
Shell erection	4 weeks
Shell enclosure and mechanical prep	3 weeks

Two Months to Ready for Trim

Mechanical rough-in	4 weeks
Insulation,	1 week
Drywall	3 weeks
Exterior finish	concurrent

Two Months to Completion

Interior trim, painting	3 weeks
Cabinets, fixtures, floor coverings	3 weeks
Clean-up and close-out	1 week
Landscaping	concurrent

Moving in

Having goals for each major phase of construction helps to keep the project's progress in perspective and establishes phase deadlines.

1. <u>Months One, Two, and Three</u>; Get the house under roof, dry, and locked.
2. <u>Months Four and Five</u>; Get drywall installed and the exterior finished.
3. <u>Months Six and Seven</u>; Get the house trimmed and decorated, the lot presentable, and an occupancy permit issued.

Meeting the major completion deadlines and the sub steps to keep the project on schedule requires that supplies be on site when needed and sub trades scheduled *in advance* without creating conflicting overlaps. This sounds difficult but most sub contractors can accurately forecast when they will complete their work, allowing you and your construction advisor to schedule follow-on tasks in advance. For example, the foundation installer can give you an approximate completion date that will allow you to order the first lumber loads and notify the framing crew of a date the job will be ready for framing with lumber waiting.

The construction calendar has cursory descriptions of each element. Additional detailed information is included in the construction guides section following the calendar. Your construction advisor will be your primary source for construction questions, but having a basic understanding of the individual steps involved will give you confidence and increase your ability to judge quality work.

Read and use the construction guides, seek your construction advisor's advice often, take progress and delivery photographs, keep your files current, deal with delays calmly, pay bills on time, and keep your project phone charged and ready.

CONSTRUCTION CALENDAR

THREE MONTHS TO DRY and SECURE
(PHASE ONE)
(House under-roof, windows and temporary exterior doors installed)

Lot clearing and excavation	2 weeks
Foundation / organizing the building site	3 weeks
Shell erection	4 weeks
Shell enclosure and mechanical preparations	3 weeks

Lot Clearing and Excavation, Two Weeks

It is essential that your property lines are accurately determined and clearly marked before you cut brush and remove unwanted trees. Avoid burial pits for trash or trash burning. Preserve topsoil if possible. Where your neighbors grass ends or a fence exists, is not an accurate indicator of a property line's actual location.

A surveyor should be engaged to mark your property lines and stake out the house to meet set back and side yard requirements and to avoid easements. A formal site plan by a registered surveyor or civil engineer may be required for a building permit. Accuracy in locating the house and accuracy in establishing its elevation relative to its surroundings is imperative. The excavator needs to know where to dig and how deep to dig within a few inches. Mistakes here are very costly and can delay or doom a project.

Use the surveyor as often as necessary. The survey instruments used by surveyors are accurate. Instruments used by excavators require frequent realignment and may not be accurate. Check the layout and elevations with the excavator and the construction advisor before digging, especially for grade, (height), at the future garage location and at other entry points to the house. Insure the security and accuracy of the benchmark the excavator is using as a reference.

When the excavator has finished digging the basement, crawl space, or trenches for a slab, have the surveyor return to check the grade and pin the corners of the footers. When the concrete footers have hardened, have the surveyor return, again, to mark the actual foundation corners with nails in the footers. These returns may not be necessary for installed precast foundations. Installers of precast basement systems use sophisticated instruments to insure accuracy and *assume responsibility* for the accuracy of their product. It is extremely important to have the house correctly placed on the lot at the correct elevation. It is also important to have a square foundation, (not skewed). An out of square foundation leads to out of square rooms and difficult fits for roof trusses, cabinetry etc.

Consider sterilizing the soil in the dig for termite protection before installing the foundation, and venting under slabs for radon.

In most situations, a temporary driveway is required. Heavy traffic between the street and the house during construction will create ruts and mud making access difficult. A heavy gravel base, starting with large stones, will provide access during the first few months and need replenished before heavy loads of basement walls or concrete trucks need access. Consecutive loads of smaller stones to repair the drive during construction will build a solid base for a concrete or asphalt drive when the house is finished.

A temporary electric power supply to the building site eliminates the need for subcontractors to bring generators to power their tools. The electrical contractor should be one of the first mechanical subcontractors chosen and should be engaged early to bring temporary electricity to the building site if possible.

Work with your Construction Advisor to keep the building site organized. Consider where material loads will be out of the way but accessible, where cranes and heavy equipment can be placed safely, where workers trucks can be parked, and where the portable-toilet should be located.

(Use your Construction Advisor)
(Refer often to construction oversight guides in part two of this section)

Install Foundation / Organize the Building Site

Three Weeks

During the design phase, you and your designer chose a foundation type and included it in your design drawings. The accuracy of installation for any type of foundation determines, in large part, the accuracy and stability of the house resting on it. The placement, grade, proper size, structural integrity, and correct angularity of the foundation will determine how well the framing crew can fit the dimensions specified in the design drawings to the foundation and what they have to adjust and approximate. Accuracy is imperative in the foundation. Have the Construction Advisor re-check grade, support post footer pad locations, anchor bolts, and overall rough dimensions. Use the surveyor as needed. An accurate foundation makes it difficult for the framing crew to make a mistake. A sloppy foundation makes it nearly impossible to avoid mistakes.

Never backfill, (push dirt back into the ditch around the new foundation), until the first floor deck is in place, and in some cases, not until the basement concrete floor has been poured. Basement walls need their tops and bottoms secured from tipping or scooting when pressure from fresh backfill material is applied.

Don't overlook basement plumbing, heating or any drain lines needed under concrete floors. Before backfilling, insure waterproofing and downspout drains are in place.

(See site visit forms Tab 6)

Organizing the Building Site

Coordinating the diverse activities involved in custom home construction begins with the selection of a building site and the placement of the home. Building on a large open property, away from property lines, trees or other obstructions allows space for construction activities. Building on a smaller wooded site imposes restrictions and requires a more organized approach.

Your construction advisor and sub trades can suggest where large deliveries need placed and how much maneuvering room large machines will need. Having an overall picture of what to place where and what areas need kept clear is important. Lot clearing opens the site for the new home and provides maneuvering room for equipment. Cranes and backhoes with a limited reach need solid ground to establish a stable base for operation. Ask your construction advisor if advanced visits by operators are advisable to determine their needs. Consider protecting nearby trees. Heavy equipment can damage trees by running over their roots, (usually extending as far as their limbs).

Another important consideration in keeping the building site operative is access. Roads leading to the building site need to be capable of carrying heavy loads and capable of accommodate tall trucks without snagging wires or tree limbs. If a culvert is required at the drive entrance, it must be wide enough and strong enough to accommodate large, heavy vehicles. During construction, the future driveway is primarily a construction access road and it will require maintenance. The construction access drive's placement and condition will, in most cases, provide the base for, and become the permanent location of your driveway. Your excavator is your best advisor for maintaining the construction access drive in a way that builds a solid base for your permanent driveway.

The excavator organizes the building site early when he grades and gravels the construction drive, clears brush, piles top soil for later use, and sets aside excavated dirt. A site visit during excavation, to identify needed future open areas for lumber and truss deliveries and for crane locations, will avoid dirt piles in the wrong place and a recall of the excavator to move them.

Final building site organization involves choices for sidewalks, patios, landscaping, driveways, parking areas, sprinkler systems, and landscape lighting. Keep next steps and final goals for the building site in mind throughout planning and construction and, with the help of subcontractors and your construction advisor the building site will stay organized.

Shell Erection, Four Weeks

The frame structure of your new home will go up quickly if,

1. the weather cooperates,
2. the foundation matches framing dimensions,
3. materials arrive when needed,
4. there are no last minuet design changes

Review your foundation drawings for any frame support walls and beams and posts needed in the basement to support the first floor above. Order these with the first lumber load or earlier.

Wood beams can be, cut to fit snuggly into beam pockets. Shortening a steel beam is difficult and lengthening any beam is impossible. Check steel beam dimensions on the blueprints against the actual foundation dimensions before they are ordered.

A thin, insulation-like, termite barrier is required on the top of basement walls before lumber is applied. Next, a treated piece of lumber, called a base plate is bolted to the foundation. The next piece of lumber, (the bottom plate of the stud wall), is nailed to the treated plate and secured to it and the foundation with clips, straps, or by overlapping wall sheathing

(See cross sections on blueprints)

If you are building a large house, multiple lumber loads will be required and specialty materials, like structural insulated panels, floor trusses, roof trusses, and laminated wood beams may come from separate suppliers. Sequencing the delivery of multiple loads to avoid delaying the framing crew and forcing them to switch to another job is essential. It is also important to avoid job site congestion by not placing loads in the way of equipment or other deliveries. Coordinating dates and placements requires anticipation and cooperation. Your construction advisor's advice will be especially valuable during this fast moving phase of construction but the best source for advice on delivery scheduling and placement is the framing crew. Other things to consider as floor and walls go up, are pocket doorframes, (which must be built-in), and large tubs and shower units that won't fit through doors or windows after the house is enclosed. Have them delivered early.

Have your construction advisor check a few rough window openings to insure they match those specified on the blueprints. If the framers are using ladders to access and move materials to upper floors, consider asking them to build a temporary set of stairs. Look for other safety items where temporary rails are needed etc. Check that backing is installed where it will be needed for drywall nailing surfaces.

Your drawings will probably specify OSB in place of plywood for floors, exterior walls and the roof. OSB stands for oriented strand board. OSB is layers of wood chips oriented in different directions bonded with permanent glue. OSB puffs when soaked but, in most cases it can be sanded flat. Wet plywood delaminates and may need replacing. Unless you are building in the dessert, your house will probably get wet before the roof is completed. The best protection for wet lumber is to allow it to dry quickly. Do this by keeping new plywood and OSB floors clean and free of sawdust and scraps. Sawdust collects in corners, holds water, and allows adjacent lumber to soak rather than dry. Keep the new frame structure clean and free of sawdust, pick up scrap lumber, and blow off any standing water. Insist that subcontractors clean up and keep the building site clear of waste and discarded materials. Hire a cleanup person if necessary, or do it yourself as a part of your site visits. A broom, a bucket, a leaf blower, and work gloves, are the only tools needed.

Your construction advisor is the best judge of quality work but, (in general), if it looks good it probably is good. Sloppy work stands out. If you see something questionable, have your construction advisor review it. Good subcontractors are competent, proud of their work, and willing to answer questions. Give compliments, and show your approval, but don't be afraid to ask dumb questions. Dumb questions are safe questions. The construction advisor is expected to know as much as the subcontractor. The owner is not. Any owner attempt to showoff with knowledge of the subcontractor's specialty will backfire.

The roof structure is the most difficult and the most dangerous part of framing. Roof trusses are large wobbly awkward items that have a tendency to fall over like dominoes until roof sheathing is in place. The slope of the roof determines difficulty. On blueprints, roof slope is designated as roof pitch and is designated as a ratio of rise to run. A 6/12 roof pitch rises six vertical feet for every twelve horizontal feet. An 8/12 pitch is the steepest pitch a person can work on without cleats and a safety harnesses. Labor costs for steep roofs are proportionally higher.

The framing crew will build the roof structure and cover it with OSB sheathing. To avoid moisture problems, small "H" clips keep a small gap between the 4' X 8' OSB sheets. Hurricane clips are required to tie trusses and other structural roof members to the house walls. Remind the framing crew to install gable louvers and vents and cut roof openings for skylights. Avoid cutting trusses and provide temporary cover over any roof openings.

If the roofing crew is not going to be immediately available, ask the framing crew to apply a temporary cover of felt to the roof as protection. In addition, ask them to tack a plastic skirt around the lower perimeter of the house to protect the foundation and the over dig from splash from roof runoff until gutters are installed. These items may have been included in their bid, if not, agree on a price and pay for them as an extra.

Shell Enclosure, Three Weeks

Have roofing applied and windows and temporary exterior doors installed as soon as possible. A dry and secure structure is a priority for any new residential structure. Being dry protects lumber from becoming wet and warping. Being secure allows indoor storage of materials and tools. Make the garage floor dry with fresh gravel or concrete for mechanical contractors to use for storage and workspace. Delay garage door installation to protect them from damage. As soon as the house is secure and locked, notify your insurance agent. Be certain your subcontractors have access.

Protect interior hardwood like oak stair treads, hardwood window seats, and interior door and window trim from damage by insuring the house is without leaks. Cover expensive stair treads and window seats to prevent scuffs and watermarks. A can of soda left overnight on a hardwood surface can leave a circular watermark that is impossible to remove.

Roofing materials require owner selections. There is a variety of roofing types, asphalt shingles (in various weights and shapes), wood shakes, slate, and metal roofing (in various profiles and colors). This is your first and most important exterior selection. If you have a definite look in mind for the exterior of your house, coordinating the many colors and selections available for roof, siding, and trim, will be easy. Collect large samples and compare them outside in natural light.

Preparing for the installation of mechanical systems

As you approach a dry and secure house, notify the mechanical contractors that the project is approaching a stage that will allow them to begin work. Give them as much lead-time as possible. They will want to review their proposals and examine the structure. They will also need to order materials, coordinate with other mechanical contractors, and adjust their schedules. Lead-time is important. The scheduling of mechanical contractors is difficult. Many things need considered including cooperation, competition and who goes first. Organizing the installation of plumbing, HVAC, electrical wiring, sound system, cable TV, built in vacuum systems, security systems, etc. is beyond an owner's or a construction advisors ability to schedule. Fortunately the various mechanical installers have stumbled over each other so often that they have sorted themselves out and know what coordination is needed and how to work around each other. Give all of them advanced notice and the phone numbers of the other mechanical contractors and they will do most of the sorting and scheduling for you.

It is important to understand that electrical, HVAC, and plumbing layouts are rarely included in residential blueprints. The reason for this is that, unlike commercial blueprints, the wiring, HVAC, and plumbing diagrams of residential projects are relatively simple and rarely followed. Residential mechanical contractors are licensed, building inspectors are both licensed and experienced, and both residential materials and methods are specified and controlled. Complex mechanical drawings are only occasionally needed in residential construction but are of little value when bypassed by experienced installers to make the system functional and approved by a building inspector as safe and adequate.

A key start to the mechanical phase is a walk-through of the framed shell of your new home with the electrician. The purpose of the walk-through is to verify the location of outlets, lighting fixtures, switches, TV cable outlets, service needed for appliances, etc. To prepare for this walk through, one set of blueprints should be marked up showing where you want, interior and exterior lighting fixtures, TV outlets, floor outlets, and any other special exterior or interior outlets for fish tanks, hobbies, kitchen appliances etc. Make a copy of your marked up blueprints for the electrician.

Code specifies wall outlet spacing and locations so only special locations need to be marked. Light switch locations can be marked but your electrician may have suggestions so ask for suggestions during the walk-through. If in doubt about an extra TV outlet, put it in, It is a lot less expensive now, than later. The electrician will have marked up his own copy of the blueprints and will probably mark on studs with a magic marker during the walk through. Don't forget the garage, the basement, any attic spaces that might be finished later. Give the electrician a copy of your marked up drawings and ask if you are still within his original bid amount.

(Use your Construction Advisor)
(Refer often to construction oversight guides in the next part)

CONSTRUCTION

CONSTRUCTION CALENDAR

TWO MONTHS TO READY FOR TRIM

Exterior finish	concurrent with interior work
Mechanical rough, heating, plumbing, electrical	4 weeks
Insulation	1 week
Drywall	3 weeks

Exterior finish, concurrent with interior work

(See personal selections checklist and deadlines Tab 5, pages 205 & 213)
(Refer often to construction oversight guides in the next part)

Finishing the exterior of a new home involves several trades and suppliers and requires many personal selections by the owner. Materials needed include,

- Exterior brick and stone
- Siding and trim
- Gutters and downspouts
- Porch posts and railings
- Louvers and shutters
- Exterior lights and brackets

Installers and subcontractors needed include,

- Masons
- Siding installers
- Gutter and downspout installers
- Carpenters
- Electricians

Coordinating color and texture selections for the exterior of your home is not easy. Try to get large samples of roofing materials, potential siding materials in various colors, and sample trim pieces in various colors. Compare them outside in natural light. Don't overlook simulated materials. Metal and vinyl simulated wood, wood shake, brick and stone, when used properly, can enhance an otherwise boring façade. Start your selections early. There may be a long lead-time for materials.

Mechanical Rough-in, Four Weeks

(See personal selections checklists Tab 5, page 205)

If you have contracted with a single company to install heating, plumbing, and electrical, they will schedule and coordinate their installation activities to avoid installation conflicts. If you have contracted with separate electrical, plumbing, and heating contractors you, with the help of your construction advisor, need to encourage cooperation between the interdependent trades, to schedule so conflicts don't occur, and to arbitrate any conflicts that do occur.

In general the more difficult it is to make installation adjustments without violating building standards or codes, the higher priority a mechanical trade has for going first. This usually puts the installation of rough plumbing first, heating ducts next and wiring last. Cooperation between mechanical trades is also necessary. Water heaters and furnaces require electrical power and plumbing drains and lines are needed near furnaces. Cooperation is also needed between mechanical trades, insulation installers, and framing requirements.

(Use your Construction Advisor)
(Refer often to construction oversight guides in the next part)

Insulation, One Week

Only after passing rough plumbing, wiring, and heating inspections, can a framing inspection take place, and only after passing a framing inspection can insulation be installed.

Codes specify the insulation requirements in your area as "R" values for walls and attics, and "U" values for windows and doors. These, along with heating and cooling efficiencies determine your homes compliance with State energy requirements. Air infiltration also contributes to a house's heat loss. Foam sealing around window and doorframes eliminates many air leaks. Eliminate other leaks by foaming around electrical outlets and wire and pipe passages through studs on exterior walls. A pressure check of the house may be required as part of the inspection process to check for excessive air infiltration.

Other areas of heat loss are through basement walls and around slab floors. Insulation not specified properly in blueprints can delay a building permit. Insulation not installed properly in these areas can cause a failed inspection and expensive corrections.

CONSTRUCTION

Drywall, Three Weeks

Only after all insulation has been installed and has been inspected, can drywall begin. On walls with studs set at 16" on-center, or on SIP, (structural insulated panel), walls, ½" drywall is sufficient. Ceilings with trusses set at 24" on center require 5/8" drywall. ¾" wood ceilings can replace drywall on high ceilings in most States. Water resistant drywall, (green) is for high moisture areas like bathrooms.

Drywall delivery trucks need to get close to the house for delivery and may require the removal of an upper window to get drywall to the second floor. To avoid delays in the drywall phase it is best to have drywall installers include materials in their bids and coordinate deliveries as needed. The installation of drywall creates a great deal of scrap. The finishing of drywall creates dust that infiltrates everything. Continual clean up during this phase is very important. To avoid dust damage block and seal ductwork and try not to heat with a new furnace.

It is common for drywall installers to complain about framing inaccuracies. If their complaints are justified, have your construction advisor check and, only if needed, call the framing crew back to make corrections. It is also common to have the painting crew complain about drywall installation. In most cases the common practice of blaming a previous trade for problems that complicate their own work, is just venting and of no real consequence but, always investigate complaints.

CONSTRUCTION CALENDAR

TWO MONTHS TO COMPLETION

(Refer often to construction oversight guides in the next part)

Interior trim, painting	2 weeks
Cabinets and counter tops	2 weeks
Plumbing fixtures	1 week
Lighting Fixtures	1 week
Floor coverings	1 week
Driveway and walkways	1 week
Clean-up, touch-up and close out	concurrent
Landscaping	concurrent

Cabinetry, countertops, appliances, floor coverings, plumbing fixtures, trim materials, interior doors, exterior doors, doorknobs, closet layouts, tile selections and lighting fixtures are all a part of this construction phase. Review your selections, if the materials can be stored, order in advance. Notify subcontractors and installers well in advance.

(See personal selections checklists Tab 5, page 205)

Interior trim, painting, Two Weeks

Painting interior walls with a coat of basic white is easy if done before baseboards and casing around doors and windows is applied. Clean and remove dust before painting. Choosing wall colors before floor coverings and furniture is in place is a bad idea. Live in your new house for a year before choosing wall colors. After living in your house for a few months, your decorating ideas will jell and you will make better choices.

The trim in your new home will be, either a composite material, or, a species of wood, (pine, oak, etc.), and will come in many profiles and sizes. Unless your house is very formal keep the trim simple and of a reasonable size. Composite materials often come pre-painted. Soft wood trim has a fine grain and may be stained or painted, painting is preferred. Hardwood trim is more expensive, looks more formal, is more difficult to work with, and has a deep grain that shows through paint. Staining is preferred. Choose an interior trim profile and size that compliments the architectural style of your house. Upgrade trim size and profile in formal rooms if desired, but do not change from painted trim to stained trim or vice-versa. Select trim species, profiles and paint or stain colors early. Most suppliers will not stock enough trim items to do a complete house and pre painting or staining will take time. Pre painting or staining a wooden wainscot or ceiling makes the work much neater and the process much easier.

Pre-painted or pre-stained trim requiring only touch up after installation makes the painting / staining process much easier.

If special built-ins, bookshelves, pre-built curved stairs, custom cabinetry etc. are a part of the project, try to match wood, stain, and paint colors if possible. Mismatched wood species and stains are usually acceptable. Mismatched paint colors stand out.

Tile backsplash, tile floors and tile showers are a part of this construction phase. Select well in advance.

Cabinets and counter tops, Two Weeks
(Review selections checklists and deadlines Tab 5, pages 205 & 213)

Have your kitchen designer or cabinetry installer measure while drywall is being taped and finished to be certain cabinets will fit as planned,. Stay ahead of potential errors.

The installation of cabinetry and counter tops is a specialty sometimes done by the cabinetry supplier and sometimes by the trim carpenter. Some cabinets will require wiring, some the installation of a sink, and others special trim. Insure wiring and plumbing is ready and located properly. Consider the height of the countertop with regard to the removal of appliances. Cabinets set on a subfloor lower than tile or wood flooring applied later under or in front of the dishwasher or refrigerator may block their installation or later removal.

Plumbing fixtures, One Week

(Review personal selections checklists Tab 5, page)

Your early plumbing fixture selections determined the location of plumbing and floor drains. If you have changed any of your selections, check with the plumber to be certain your new selection will fit with the now installed rough plumbing.

Your plumber may be able to buy plumbing fixtures at wholesale prices and scheduling is easier when an installer is responsible for the delivery of the items they install. Subcontractors charge for any finance and carrying charges incurred and for overhead and handling costs. When these charges are reasonable, the subcontractor's purchasing advantage may offset their additional up-charges. In general, it is to the owner's advantage to let subcontractors handle material scheduling and delivery without making them responsible for carrying the cost of materials. Small mom and pop plumbing companies will welcome an offer by owners to purchase large plumbing fixtures. Many of these items are personal selections. Be certain to coordinate closely with the plumber. Examine all delivered items as accurate, for damage, and for missing items. Photograph discrepancies.

CONSTRUCTION

Lighting fixtures, One Week

Whenever possible have the lighting fixture supplier install the fixtures they supply. The liability for dropping an expensive chandelier by the supplier during installation belongs to the supplier, and the supplier should replace it at no cost. If, however, the electrician drops the fixture a question develops as to who is liable, the electrician or the owner who directed the electrician to hang the chandelier. If possible, install expensive lighting fixtures after the installation of floor coverings to lessen the chance of breakage. If however, a final inspection and occupancy permit deadline exists, all lighting outlets must have a bulb of some kind in place, floor coverings normally need not be in place.

(Refer often to construction oversight guides in the next part)

Floor coverings, One Week

Before installing floor coverings and cove moldings, a through cleaning is important. Any debris, dirt, or dust on sub floors or in corners, will interfere with solid flooring installations and become trapped under soft floor coverings. Pay special attention to any drywall dust hiding in closets, on windowsills, etc. In general, it is best to install hardwood and tile floors before laying carpet.

Driveway and walkways, One Week

For nearly seven months, your driveway has been gravel compressed by heavy truck traffic. Your excavator now needs to return and dress up the drive, add a final small stone gravel base and prepare it for a cover of concrete or blacktop. At the same time the excavator should prepare sidewalks, dress the lot for landscaping and replace any top soil put aside earlier.

Clean-up and close out, Concurrent with other work

Interior clean up will be much easier if a clean worksite has been a priority throughout the construction process. Check drains for scrap that may have fallen in during construction. Remove as much dust as possible. Remove scraps from the area around the house and look for loose nails and fasteners in the dirt with a strong magnet. These can become dangerous projectiles when lawnmowers are used.

Final inspections are required for plumbing, heating and electrical before a final occupancy inspection. You can expect a few overlooked items that require a call back of some subcontractors but, if you have withheld a final payment for their services, they should return quickly to help you with a final close out. *Do not move any personal items into your new home before you have an occupancy permit.*

Change any locks made available to workers during construction, pay final bills, close out and consolidate your files, transfer your construction photos to a disc, roll up your approved house plans. Store all your construction records in a permanent place. Keep your project phone and construction address active for six months. Notify your insurance company, close out or convert your construction loan, notify utilities and keep heavy trucks off your new drive until given the OK by the driveway installer.

Landscaping, Concurrent with other work

Building departments do not generally have any jurisdiction over lot improvements other than utility connections. Health departments supervise septic systems and wells. Local zoning regulations dictate distances from right-of-ways, property lines and easements and often dictate storm water drainage around a new dwelling. Neighborhood organizations may however, specify minimum landscaping requirements. If the landscaping involves piecemeal work by several contractors, acquaint yourself' with all applicable rules and carefully supervise the work. If a single professional landscaper is employed it is their responsibility to comply with all requirements and restrictions.

Move-in Advice

Furniture move-in is nearly impossible without a few nicks and dings. Expect them, and have the painter leave paint and stain leftovers for repairs. You can also expect to find errors and omissions as you use the many aspects of your new home for the first time. *There is no perfect new home.* You will find things that stick, squeak, are not fastened, and don't work. If you expect this, there will be less angst. Make a list of minor items and let the items accumulate. Call your primary subcontractors back only for major errors or omissions. Fix what you can yourself or call a handy man to fix all the things on your list. The construction advisor or a competent handy man can also be a good choice to finish your basement, or to build shelves or a workbench in your garage. Hired to do these things, he may be willing fix a loose doorknob without charge.

Send thank you notes to your Construction Advisor, neighbors, suppliers, subcontractors, and the officials and inspectors that made your new home possible. If you are going to host a house warming, thank you notes can also be invitations.

CONSTRUCTION

CONSTRUCTION

PART 2
CONSTRUCTION OVERSIGHT

Construction oversight guides are general in nature. Becoming fully informed on every aspect of residential construction would take years of study and it is unrealistic to expect owners to inspect work accurately or discuss construction details intelligently. To assist owners in construction management, construction advisors bring years of construction experience to the project and give owners confidence and support. Important construction details are included in part 1 of this section to give owners perspective. The oversight guides in this part are primarily scheduling and behavioral management suggestions that owners can use to promote a smooth flow of work and cooperation between trades.

CONSTRUCTION OVERSIGHT GUIDES

Working with your Construction Advisor

Site Visits

Scheduling

Financial Management

Keeping Accurate Records

Working With Your Construction Advisor

How you, the owner/manager of your new home project, interact with your construction advisor on a daily bases is, spelled-out in the *Owner/ Construction Advisor Agreement.* How you relate to your construction advisor is not explicit in the agreement, but is just as important.

As an owner/ manager, you set the tone for all work on your project including the attitude and commitment of your construction management partner, the construction advisor. Most of the labor and material components of your project are informal contracted arrangements with basic responsibilities understood as implicit. Long legal documents spelling out every detail of how, when, and to what standards work will be done is common in large commercial projects but is rare in single-family residential projects. As the project manager, you sign the checks and, with the help of your construction advisor, schedule deliveries, schedule work, and provide quality control. Unlike the manager of a company whose employees are loyal, in part, because they are income dependent, your, one time, part time, providers of labor and materials, have other responsibilities and income sources. They require a different management style. This is especially true of your key contracted management assistant, your construction advisor.

Treated badly or having their work unfairly impugned, a subcontractor can walk away and take on another project. Your construction advisor is no different and unfairly criticized, can walk away. The secret to insuring a full commitment to your project by sub trades, suppliers, and your construction advisor is to develop a team attitude that includes pride in their work and the house they are building. The best way to accomplish this is by expressing enthusiasm, a real interest in work as it progresses, and a sincere appreciation of work accomplished. Ask your construction advisor important questions before approaching a subcontractor, especially about quality of work. Ask your construction advisor his or her opinion often. Thank him or her often for their support and let them know how much you appreciate their help, especially when they have helped you avoid or solve a problem. Do not undermine one trade by discussing their work with another trade or undermine the authority of your construction advisor by discussing their advice or instructions with a sub trade.

Confer with your construction advisor often but do not become a pest. Be considerate of their other obligations and of their family time. Use text messages for simple concerns, voice calls for more urgent matters, and try to accomplish most of your important interactions during mutual visits to the building site. Acknowledge every required report immediately with a response or a thank you. Responding immediately lets them know you are paying attention. It also lets them know that any missed reports will be noticed.

It is not necessary or advisable that you become good friends with your construction advisor. A good working relationship is essential and an occasional show of appreciation is appropriate. Attitude is essential in determining the success of a single-family custom home project. Working in the wind, in the heat, and in the mud is very different from working in an office or a factory. Down time caused by missing or late material deliveries cost subcontractors money and degrades their attitude. A nervous or angry owner or construction advisor also degrades attitude. On time deliveries and a clean safe and comfortable work site improves attitude, as does enthusiasm and praise from the owner and construction advisor.

Managing your construction advisor and successfully scheduling and managing the flow of supplies and succession of assembly tasks is primarily a matter of self management, of organization, and attitude control.

Stay accessible, organized, calm, enthusiastic, and somewhat self-deprecating and your relationship with your construction advisor will be one of mutual respect and cooperation.

Site Visit Guides
(See Forms Tab 6, page 230)

Dress appropriately for visits to the building site, and use extreme caution. Construction sites are dangerous and are inappropriate for children.

The purpose of a joint site visit is for the construction advisor to asses the project and for the owner to receive advice and assurance from the construction advisor. Joint visits also provide the owner an opportunity to ask questions about quality of work.

The purpose of an owner only site visit, without the construction advisor, is to praise good work, determine when next work can begin, when to order next deliveries, and to asses the site's cleanliness and safety.

Site visits are essential and, in part, determine the attitude and success of the project. Primary site visits are those made by the construction advisor and building inspectors to insure progress and compliance. Secondary visits are those made by the owner to assure the owner of adequate progress, allow the owner to show enthusiasm and, to help the owner coordinate personal selections. Owners should never discuss questions they may have regarding faulty construction with subcontractors or tradesmen. Reserve such questions for the construction advisor.

During an owner only site visit, a subcontractor or tradesman may suggest a change or ask the owner a question. Suggestions may involve only the use of a new material or a new assembly method or it may involve a departure from the blueprints. Suggestions may be good and improve the design or be inappropriate. All suggestions, good or bad, demand serious consideration and the owner must consult the construction advisor and sometimes the Designer before approving or disapproving any changes. An inconsiderate dismissal of a suggestion made by a tradesman who takes enough interest in the project to offer a suggestion will affect attitudes adversely. Even suggestions made only to make a tradesman's job easier need consideration and deserve a respectful reply. A first consideration for any change is its effect on other aspects of the design. Similarly, any questions asked of the owner regarding blueprint interpretation, materials, or construction methods, need the input of the construction advisor. Reciprocally, suggestions and questions made to the construction advisor must be coordinated with the owner.

Owners unfamiliar with the changing perspectives of a home under construction can easily misinterpret the size of the house and the size of rooms at various stages of construction. The home's blueprints impart mental images to the owner different from listed dimensions. Imagined room sizes may not match the real image seen during a site visit. The actual foundation often seems considerably smaller that what the owner imagined. Before drywall is applied, stud walls make rooms seem smaller than imagined. With Drywall applied, before doors or trim is in place, rooms seem larger than imagined. Only when drywall, doors and trim are in place do rooms acquire a size and proportion close to the owner's mental image. Owners should expect these differing perspectives to occur when they confirm blueprint dimensions.

Frequent site visits are essential to determine actual project progress, which in turn determines the construction schedule, material delivery schedules, and owner selections. Adjust the construction calendar to meet actual progress to keep guidance current.

(See "Owner Site Visit" checklist, Tab 6, page 230)

CONSTRUCTION

Guides for Scheduling

During the construction phase, the scheduling of work and deliveries will be the owner's most difficult and time-consuming activity. To allow subcontractors to adjust their schedules and suppliers to assemble and order materials, *schedule in advance* Stay well ahead of actual construction. The construction calendar provides scheduling guides but actual scheduling depends on actual progress. The basement can't be set until a hole is ready, and framing can't begin until the basement is finished, etc. Copy and post *the construction calendar,* and *the selections deadline checklist* for easy reference near the spot in your home or office you have reserved for project management. Mark estimated completion dates on the calendars for each task as soon as they can be determined.

To allow subcontractors to adjust their schedules, and to be certain they are still available, keep all your subcontractors informed of the projects progress. Check often on deadlines for materials that need assembly before they can be delivered, (precast basement systems, roof trusses, curved stairs, etc.). Check often on lead-times for items that are special orders, (steel beams, I Joists, special doors, etc.). Call months ahead to avoid missing a lead-time that can delay the project. An alternate purchase can sometimes overcome a delay when a noncritical material becomes unavailable or will cause a delay. Oversights in the timely scheduling of critical labor segments, however, are more difficult to overcome and can cause lengthy delays.

The sequentially dependant chain of subcontracted work is the primary determinant of how smoothly and how quickly the entire project will proceed to a successful conclusion. Make a list of the, ("can't start" until "this is finished") chain of labor events. Off to the side, make another list of the materials each link in the chain needs to complete its task. The thought needed to make this list is more important than the list itself. Making the list should take only fifteen minuets, but the effort focuses your attention on the key scheduling events important for a smooth flow of work.

Regular site visits and many phone calls, along with focus is needed to schedule work and materials. If your project phone has all the important numbers, and if your files are current, scheduling will be easy.

Guide to Keeping Accurate Records

Accurate record keeping was important in the planning and pricing phase and is even more important during the construction phase. Record the details of every site visit on your project phone and as dated entries in your construction computer. Record every phone call with date, time and details as a written record. Keep dated photos of site visits by your construction advisor, especially photos of deliveries. Transfer and keep all of your construction advisor's text reports. Detailed records will help with scheduling, with financing, and can become essential for an insurance claim, to resolve a dispute, or if a theft occurs. Do not miss recording important information. Be obsessive in recording details. It will keep you focused, will avoid delays, and save money.

Financial Management Suggestions

After five months of selecting and purchasing a building site, paying for design work, arranging a construction loan, setting up a project bank account for miscellaneous expenses, and making initial payments to a construction advisor, your accounting system is either well established or in disarray. Assuming you and your construction lender have a workable system in place, and that your project records are in order, there is little additional advice needed, except to emphasize that a custom home project consists of dozens of contracted labor costs and hundreds of individual material costs. The goal for an on-budget custom home project is to have the final cost of every labor and material segment match its bid or estimate. The chances of this happening are zero, but If you estimated well and included taxes and a contingencies pad, over and under estimates should balance out putting you close to budget

A review of these checklists provides an overview of the many separate costs that make up the total cost of your project.

See Tab 5 for:

- Pricing Percentages
- Subcontractors Required
- Material Suppliers Required
- Owner Selections Required

Original estimates or bids will rarely match actual costs exactly and partial payments may be required.

The only way to determine an approximate current financial status for the project during construction, is to track "over and under" payments on completed aspects to see if the project as a whole is running "over or under" budget. A detailed cost estimate was probably required by your construction lender and, depending on the lenders disbursement methods, their loan statements may help as an indicator of where the project stands financially.

The secret to keeping track of the projects financial status is the same secret needed to manage the project successfully, keep accurate records!

REFERENCES SECTION

REFERENCE 1

BUILDING SITES

CREATING A BUILDING SITE SEARCH CRITERIA
EVALUATING POTENTIAL BUILDING SITES
BUILDING SITE RESTRICTIONS AND APPROVALS

CREATING A BUILDING SITE SEARCH CRITERIA

If the *where to build* question has already been answered, you don't need the first part of this guide, but the guides for evaluating potential building sites and for site restriction should still be of value.

If you are planning to build close to where you currently live, the advantages and disadvantages of location have already been experienced and accepted. It is still wise to review a predetermined site using the same criteria you would use to evaluate a new site. Your building site won't move geographically but it will move through time. Your employment may change, the schools you and your children attend will change, acceptable travel to medical and shopping may change, and your family will change. Look forward in time five years to establish your housing needs, then look forward ten years and adjust your design expectations to accommodate anticipated changes using the criteria listed below.

If you are actively seeking a suitable place to build a new home, the suggestions for establishing a search criteria listed below will help you focus on important issues. Defining the parameters for the building site you want also helps those assisting you. A poorly directed search allows the agendas of others to skew your options. A focused search presents the best options and allows you make wise choices.

CREATING A BUILDING SITE SEARCH CRITERIA

Make a Map

1. Purchase a large map of the general search area and a simple compass (circle maker)
2. Locate the anchor points of your search. (These can be addresses of key family members, a work location, a college campus, airports etc.)
3. Determine how far you are willing to travel on a regular basis to get to and from the anchor points. Use the scale listed on the map. (usually in miles)
4. Draw overlapping travel limit circles on the map using the anchor points as the centers.
5. Highlight acceptable travel routes, the location of preferred schools, shopping areas, hospitals and other preferences.
6. Make several copies of the search map you have created at Staples or Kinkos. Leave peripheral areas on the map as options just in case you have overlooked a good area.
7. Share copies of your map with realtors or friends helping you with your search.

CREATING A BUILDING SITE SEARCH CRITERIA

Make a List

1. List other proximity requirements that will help realtors and others select acceptable building-site options. *Special schools, an athletic facility, etc*
2. List your utility preferences. (city-water, gas, sewer, etc.)
3. Describe your vision of the building-site you are looking for. (Trees, view, open space, neighbors, hillside, flat, etc.)
4. List your vision of the neighborhood you want to build in.
5. List the price range of other homes you want around you.
6. List the general price range of the property you are looking for. For large properties, this may have no relationship to the price range of the home you want to build. For smaller lots be realistic. Developed lots can be 25% to 35% of the cost of an acceptable new home for the area. Do phone research to arrive at a realistic price range.

EVALUATING POTENTIAL BUILDING SITES

As you create a portfolio of potential building sites, you will learn a great deal about the general area that will further refine your search. To save time, eliminate unacceptable sites early. Visit every potential site and walk the property. Explore the surrounding area, notice the neighbors, be cognizant of where the sun comes up and where it sets, be aware of adjacent roads or factory noises, of prevailing wind directions, smells, potential flood areas, the view, where your driveway will most likely be located and where your house will probably set. Ask about schools, taxes, the proximity of emergency services and local soil conditions as they relate to foundations and septic systems etc. As you narrow your search to a few potential sites, ask more specific questions related to building restrictions, such as home size restrictions, style requirements etc.

Most of the rules and restrictions related to building sites become obvious when you become serious about a particular site. A subdivision that requires all two-story homes to be over 3,500 sq feet may exceed your intentions and eliminate the site immediately. Only a few planning restrictions are subtle enough to be missed so don't be too concerned about making a mistake. If you are still nervous after examining all the information available for a particular site, see if you can secure a first option on the property that will cover the duration of the design phase. If this option is available, you can reduce the risk of owning a building site you later find unsuitable. Judge the property on its own merits. Most good building sites are good investments even if you never build on them.

When you get close to a final selection, engage either the services of a home designer to examine the compatibility between the home you want and the lot you have selected, or engage a competent builder to evaluate the compatibility between a selected house plan and the building-site. Sometimes it is necessary to risk a deposit on the land while final evaluations or soils testing takes place. During compatibility checks between the building site and the house you want, continue your efforts to learn more about local building restrictions that may affect your house design.

(See Building Site Evaluation Checklist Tab 5, page)

BUILDING SITE RESTRICTIONS AND APPROVALS

As you evaluate prospective building sites for compatibility, with the house you intend to build, locate all the restrictions that may apply. You probably won't have a set of house plans at this stage, but you should have an idea of the style and size of the house you want. Check your vision against the restrictions that come with the building site before you commit.

Before you purchase a building site, attempt to acquire all applicable regulations, requirements, and building restrictions that will affect or restrict what you can build. The rules are established and enforced by associations and agencies that include;

- Homeowner's associations, (architectural style and other requirements),
- The local Health Department, (for well or septic system permits),
- The Parish, Township or County, (for zoning permits),
- The County or City, (for building permits),
- The State, (for highway or road access permits),
- Various corporate engineering departments, (sewer, water, and gas tap-in requirements),
- Miscellaneous agencies, (watershed, drainage, archeological), and various utility companies, (electric, gas, water, cable, etc).

Pay special attention to deed restrictions or subdivision rules that specify minimum square footage, set back limits from the right of way, side and back yard limitations, maximum height restrictions, as well as style requirements imposed by a homeowner's association.

At first glance, the number of agencies and rules may seem overwhelming but they fall into place quickly and will start to make sense if you break them into four groups.

1. Real estate
2. Government agencies
3. Utility companies
4. Neighborhood restrictions

Real estate related rules are usually available from the person who is selling the property or from the developer or a homeowners association. A few phone calls should put the deed restrictions and lot parameters in your file.

Government agencies, on the other hand, can invent more restrictions than would seem possible. It would be a monumental task to find all of the applicable rules except for the fact that each agency nearly always requires a prerequisite approval from another agency. By establishing prerequisite approvals, they form themselves into a chain of approvals with each link easily locatable by starting at either end and working toward the other. To be certain you have started at an end link it is often easiest to start at the final permit required, usually the building permit, and work backwards. A frustrating hour on the phone will usually locate all the government agencies you will need.

Make a list of all the utilities you will need connected to your new home. Get out the phone book and contact each utility company. Tell them you are designing a new home to be built at _____ and need to know if there are any restrictions or permits you should consider during the design process. If you get someone who has no clue, ask for the engineering department. Remember you are not seeking a permit at this point. You want restrictions and information so that you plan and design within the parameters they require. Most will be able to answer your questions over the phone. A few may require additional details and a very few may request a meeting once you have plans and placement information ready.

Take the time to familiarize yourself with both the man-made rules and the natural restrictions that will shape and limit your design. If you do this, the design effort will be simplified, will result in a well-prepared project, will result in a better fit with natural surroundings, and most important, a better match with your families needs and tastes.

The "building site evaluation checklist", may seem daunting but it usually only takes a dozen or so phone calls and a few meetings to determine if a site meets your requirements. A thorough investigation also establishes valuable local contacts that can be of help later and may become new neighborhood friends. Keep track of all your contacts and the information obtained. Do not rush through these important steps. Purchasing a building site that turns out to be incompatible with your plans or has a hidden expense for a sewer hook up, (like drilling under a road), can be a problem. Do not rely on realtors to have the answers you need. Very few realtors are experienced in evaluating or trained to evaluate raw land. Do your homework. This is where you are going to live.

TAB 2

READING AND USING BLUEPRINTS

The term, "blueprint" became popular before the invention of modern copy machines. Before black and white copies, a chemically treated paper, sensitive to ultraviolet light, passed through a machine with a transparent drawing on top. The light in the machine shined through the transparent original and, except where the lines on the drawing above shaded the paper, turned the treated paper blue. The shaded lines remained white. Later, an improved process used ultraviolet light to burned-off a yellow chemical on the copy paper except where the lines on the original shaded the chemical. In this process, the remaining yellow lines on the copy paper turned blue and became permanent when subjected to an ammonia gas in another part of the copy machine. As a result, all early copies were, at first, white lines on a blue background and later, blue lines on a white background, and the term "blueprint" became popular.

Words often fall short as a way of exchanging ideas during the design process. They play a vital role, but cannot always fully describe an architectural detail. Drawings will play a central role in the exchange of ideas between you and your designer and later between you and your contractors and suppliers. If you are primarily verbal, it may be difficult for you to read the lines on the blueprints and the words and numbers may be confusing. One way to learn to read the lines is to blank out all the words on a copy of a preliminary plan. This forces you to look only at what the lines are presenting.

There is a difference between a good set of blueprints and a fancy set of blueprints. A good set of blueprints describes and depicts the house accurately and in just enough detail for everyone to know what the designer has in mind and how to put the materials together. A fancy set of blueprints is a very impressive array of renderings, complex layouts and schematics that might get an "A" in an architectural class but complicates the building process. When residential blueprints are overdrawn and excessively detailed it is often because the designer was trained primarily in commercial design, where detail is a requirement, or because it is easier to charge a high price for complicated drawings than for something that appears simple and straight forward.

There is a difference between commercial design standards and residential design standards. Detailed plumbing details, heating duct layouts, electrical plans, reflected ceiling drawings, and long lists of codes and specifications are not normally included in residential designs. Excessive details and specifications in a residential set of drawings drive bids up considerably. Your building department should have a list of minimum requirements for house plans. Some additional details may be needed, but a 20 sheet set of drawings when only five sheets are need, will result in confusion, higher costs, and cause many competent smaller construction firms to avoid bidding. Keep in mind that the drawings and specifications for a new home have only one real purpose—to communicate information. First, to communicate with you so you know what you are getting and second, to communicate with suppliers and tradesmen so they know what to supply and build.

Tips for Reading Blueprints

Digital copying now allows large sheet copies to be made from an original drawing or from a copy and drawings can be and stored in several digital formats. Copies of your house plans can be e-mailed to suppliers and contractors anywhere in the US directly, or by sending a copy to *printme@staples.com* or, *printandgo@kinkos.com* Full size copies work best. Working from a computer screen invites errors.

Professional standards and convention has established the standard methods of presentation used today and has created the common look of residential plans. Before CAD, *computer aided design/drafting*, house plans were drawn using pencil and ink on transparent paper. When plans were drawn using a straight edge and a pencil the drafting equipment was a natural extension of the designers hands and presented few distractions from the creative process. With the advent of CAD, the equipment interface became more complex. CAD requires formal training and has become a distraction as the designer tries to integrate structure, appearance and functionality into a design while manipulating a computer program. As a result, modern designs have become more sterile and less integrated. A good example is the exquisite designs produced by Scholz Homes during the 1970s by a talented single designer and the flood of look-alike computerized plans you find in many of today's magazines. Computer generated plans have nearly perfect drafting and paper presentation but lack the character of the designs from Scholz. Computer design has become the standard and has advantages, especially in the hands of a true professional, but most architects and professional designers still sketch out their original design ideas using a pencil and then turn to a computer to produce final drawings. Both methods have advantages and disadvantages depending on the designer's skill. Consider both approaches when choosing a designer.

Look for hidden problems in magazine house plans and mail order plans. CAD conversions of pencil drawings may appear modern but may be outdated and need adjustments to meet modern building codes. You should always have purchased plans reviewed by a professional before you distribute them for bids or submit them for a permit. Modern CAD drawings can also contain design errors, especially those produced from simplistic off the shelf programs done by an inexperienced designer. The drafting may look great but the structure can be unsound. One way to tell if a design is the result of a computer program and lacks careful structural considerations is to look at or ask for a structural roof plan. Most inexpensive programs default to a hip roof system without regard to needed interior support walls or bearing points and have a complete disregard for maximum allowable rafter or ceiling joist spans. The roof and the foundation require careful comparison as any plan is developed. Off-the-shelf design programs default to simple internal solutions that may or may not be realistic.

All house plans, except rough initial sketches, are *to scale*. What this means is that all plans are drawn using a reduction *constant* that will keep everything proportional. A full-scale drawing would be actual size and require very large pieces of paper. Making the drawings ½ the size of the real house doesn't help much. Making them 1/50th size would get down to paper size but be very confusing when one tries to measure something on the drawing. The accepted reduction "constant" in creating house plans is to make 1 foot on the real house equal a part of an inch on the drawings. The most common reduction is for ¼" on the drawing to represent one foot for the actual house. Other scales you will see are 1'=1/8" and 1'=1/2". Using a conventional ruler to measure things on the drawings is a chore and creates errors. Stop by the nearest office supply store and ask for an inexpensive architect's scale, a triangular scale that has the various architectural scales marked. Turn the scale to match the scale noted on the drawing. To measuring from one side of a room on the drawings to the other side, put the zero on the line on one side of the room. If the line on the other side of the room falls somewhere between 12 and 13 feet on the scale, slide the scale forward to put 12 feet on the line and look back at the other end. Zero will no longer be on the line, but you can count the little hash marks to find that the room is *approximately* 12 feet 8 inches wide.

Use caution when determining dimensions by measuring the plans. When dimensions are available they always take precedent. Room sizes written on a floor plan as (Bedroom #2 - 12 X 12) are always approximate. The only accurate dimensions are those with an associated dimension line with both of its ends identified by an arrow or a slash mark. Other accurate dimensions are a specified rough opening for windows and doors and dimensions on detailed cross sections. Measuring distances on the plans using an architect's scale can be useful but can also be erroneous and create problems. CAD programs and designers may draw to scale but paper shrinks and expands with changes in humidity and temperature and copy machines do not always copy to an exact scale. These errors can be compounded and create erroneous measurements when scaling off the plans. Before you use your architects scale to measure something on a blueprint, look for a numbered dimension and insist that your sub-trades do the same. The numbered dimension may be on a different page or on the other side of the drawing. If you can't find it, try to use other dimensions to arrive at it by adding or subtracting.

One reason a dimension may be missing is that the designer has intentionally omitted it. For example, some designers show overall dimensions only on the foundation plan, knowing that as lumber is applied above, the lumber will have to fit the reality of the foundation not the drawings and, if there is a discrepancy, it will force a look at the foundation plan not an unacceptable compromise in framing dimensions. Another reason to omit a dimension is to insure that small dimensional adjustments are made in noncritical areas. There is occasionally a series of end-to-end dimensions across the entire drawing where some of the dimensions are critical and some that can vary slightly without creating a serious structural effect. The designer may omit noncritical dimensions so that if layout adjustments are required, they will be made in a non dimensioned-noncritical area.

Residential blueprints have five common elements.

1. Foundation Plans (Plans are flat views from above)
2. Floor Plans
3. Elevations (Elevations are flat views from the side)
4. Structural, Details and Cross Sections
5. Roof Plan

Common to all house plans are the floor plans. Floor plans are a type of cross section. Visualize a scale model of your design setting on the floor with you standing directly over it looking down on the roof. Now take a sharp knife and with the blade parallel to the floor slice through the model about half way up the first floor walls. Next lift off the top half of the model and set it aside. You are now looking down on the first floor of your design with the roof and the upper half of the walls missing. You can see the rooms, the walls, where the windows and doors are located and other items such as kitchen cabinets, appliances, and plumbing fixtures. Plans for second and third floors work the same way. Floor plans that aren't excessively cluttered with dimensions and other written information should allow you to visualize traffic flow, furniture placement, and room sizes. Pay particular attention to wall space for beds, and traffic flow near entry doors and through living rooms. Ceiling details are rarely indicated on residential house plans, but varying ceiling heights and styles can add very dramatic effects. Use caution. Unless the overall design accommodates special ceiling details easily, they can be problematic.

Long arrows on the basement plan indicate the directions and spacing of the floor joists holding up the first floor. First floor joists are shown on the basement plan so the basement walls and beams supporting them can be visualized. Likewise, second floor joists are shown on the first floor plan so first floor support walls can be identified. The long arrows indicating joist directions are annotated with the size and type of joist to be used. An example is, (2 X 10 @ 16" OC over), meaning two by ten inch floor joists placed at sixteen inches on center. Purchased plans and beginner design programs often overlook or exceed span limitations for standard lumber.

Exterior elevations are also common to all house plans. These flat, one dimensional, views give you a good idea of what your house will look like from the outside. Keep in mind that they are a flat, straight on perspectives of each side of your house as viewed from a level point half way up the wall. The actual house will look slightly taller from ground level and different from other perspectives. Use your imagination to create these views. Three-dimensional presentations can sometimes help but they can also mislead, especially if they are an artists rendering similar to those accompanying offerings in magazines.

The foundation plan for your new home is the house's *footprint.* A quick comparison between the footprint of a ranch design and the footprint of a two-story design with a similar amount of living area will reveal a much larger footprint for the ranch. The roof of a ranch design is also considerably larger than on a two-story house. This is why ranch designs are more expensive than two story designs. Three story designs are even less expensive and five story row houses in Philadelphia even less expensive. The first function of any foundation is to carry the total weight of the house and spread the weight on the ground under the house so it will remain stable for many years. The second function of the foundation is to carry the weight deep enough so that the earth it is resting upon will always be below any freezing ground. Freezing ground can lift the foundation. The foundation plan is the best place to look for the overall dimensions for the size of your house. A good design will have dimensions in even feet or dimensions of even feet plus 4" or 8" Foundations with dimensions in odd inches or fractions of inches may occur in designs with odd angles but, in rectangular designs, odd dimensions are usually an indication that the designer is using a beginners CAD program. The basement plan must show major beams and post supports.

Structural and construction details are included in house plans as instructions for builders and to inform building officials that building codes and safe practices will be followed. Some of these will be enlarged details of difficult layout areas and some will be cross sections, (vertical slices through walls and rooms showing how construction materials fit together). Building codes change rapidly and these details are often outdated in purchased plans. Unless you are building a very large, expensive home, excessive inclusions of window, door and trim details are also an indication that plans are outdated, or are excessively detailed to justify high design costs.

An important dimensional detail shown on residential plans is the rough opening size for windows and doors. Doors come in common sizes and, unless you need special doors, will be designated by their common widths and assume a standard height of 6'-8". Windows, on the other hand, must meet egress and size requirements for various rooms and, depending on the manufacturer, will require different sized wall openings. Most architects use a window and door schedule, (a list of all the windows with a code number or letter on the floor plans showing where they go and how big the rough opening must be for the window to fit. Others prefer to have the owners select the window manufacture they want to use in advance and list the window designation and the rough opening directly on the floor plans eliminating the need for the framing crew to flip back and forth between the window schedule and the floor plan during construction.

A roof plan *with structural details* is essential in all residential house plans. Engineered roof trusses have replaced ceiling joists and rafters because they allow longer ceiling spans and larger rooms. The steepness of the roof has a great deal to do with the appearance of the house and with the cost. A pitch of 4 feet in every twelve feet, (4/12) is about minimum to prevent water from creeping up between shingles and an 8/12 pitch is about the limit for work without scaffolding. Roof overhang distances may be limited in steep pitches to avoid conflict with the tops of windows. There is a lot to consider in a custom home design. The help of a professional is advisable. Off-the shelf design packages are discouraged.

Alternate building materials are becoming common and traditional trade skills are becoming less common. Designing with Structural Insulated Wall Panels, Precast Foundations, Floor Trusses, and many more options are available. On the other hand, finding a plasterer or competent mason is becoming problematic. During the planning stage of your custom home, you may have to choose between a poured concrete foundation, a block foundation or a Superior Wall foundation. Use the internet to educate yourself. Concrete block foundations are cheap, poured wall foundations are strong and if you are planning a finished basement, a Superior Wall system is a good option, see *mybasement. com*. Old timers will have one opinion, younger designers and builders will have another.

Using Blueprints to Estimate Materials

Construction material estimating and pricing requires time and effort and is not necessary for a successful project. Material estimating can, however save money when done prior to actual bidding. Knowing the cost of materials allows owners to evaluate material bids and to estimate labor, overhead, and profit markups in combined labor and material bids.

Construction drawings are drawn to scale, (can be measured), and contain cross sections detailing the type of materials needed. This combination allows you to determine the quantities and kinds of materials required for construction. The common scale reduction used in residential house plans is, ¼" = 1', (one fourth of an inch on the drawings equals one foot on the actual house). Using an architects (¼" triangular scale) to measure, (a ruler requires you to count and convert inches and is not suitable), and the formula in Tab 7, you can make reasonable estimates of the construction materials needed for your new home. Using "on-line" prices from Big Box retailers, you can then, estimate the cost of most of the construction materials you will need. If your blueprints are drawn to 1/8"=!' take them to a copy center and have them enlarged by 100%. A 1/8" scale is too small to measure accurately.

TAB 3

CONTACT LISTS AND PHONE SCRIPTS

*IMPORTANT CONTACTS LIST

*CONSTRUCTION ADVISOR INTERVIEW

*PHONE SCRIPTS

CALLING GUIDES TO LOCATE <u>SUBCONTRACTORS</u>

See also Subcontractors Needed Checklist (Tab 5, page 201)

REFERENCES 3

CALLING GUIDES TO LOCATE <u>MATERIAL SUPPLIERS</u>

(See also Material Suppliers Needed Checklist Tab 5, page 203)

REFERENCES 3

IMPORTANT CONTACTS LIST

Emergency

(those servicing the area of the new home)

Fire _____

Police _____

Ambulance _____

Animal Control _____

Inspection, Financial, Insurance, Government

Zoning Inspector _____

Health Department _____

Building Department _____

Insurance Agent _____

Construction Lender _____

Bank _____

Other _____

Other _____

ADVISORY CONTACTS

Designer / Architect _____

Project Advisor _____

Building Inspector _____

Other _____

_____

UTILITY COMPANY CONTACTS

Electric _____

Water _____

Gas _____

Cable _____

Other _____

Other _____

SUBCONTRACTOR CONTACTS

Well _____

Septic _____

Excavator _____

Electrical _____

Concrete work _____

Masonry / Foundation _____

Framing _____

Roofing _____

Siding _____

Plumbing _____

Heating Cooling _____

Insulation _____

Drywall _____

Trim Carpentry _____

Cabinet Installer _____

Painting _____

Flooring _____

Other _____

Other _____

CONSTRUCTION MATERIAL SUPPLIER CONTACTS

Gravel _____

Concrete _____

Lumber _____

Windows / Doors _____

Roofing _____

Trim Materials _____

Other _____

_____

_____

OWNER SELECTIONS SUPPLIER CONTACTS

Brick/Stone Facing _____

Exterior Doors _____

Garage Doors _____

Siding _____

Roofing Materials _____

Plumbing Fixtures _____

Cabinetry _____

Counter Tops _____

Appliances _____

Floor Coverings _____

Exterior Lighting Fixtures _____

Interior Lighting Fixtures _____

Other _____

Other _____

CONSTRUCTION ADVISOR PHONE INTERVIEW GUIDE

Before making calls to prospective Construction Advisors, review part 2 *Using a Construction Advisor* in Construction/Construction Guides, and *Construction Advisor Agreement* in Tab 6, Forms

Date _____ Phone # _____

Prospects Name _____

Referred by _____

Address _____
(Distance from job site)

_____

Introduce yourself to the prospective Construction Advisor, explain who referred you, and explain that you are having a custom home designed, where it will be built, and that you are looking for an experienced general contractor/builder to act as a Construction Advisor.

Hello, my name is _____

XXXXXX_____ referred you as an experienced residential builder/contractor.

I am having a new home designed that will be built in

(location) _____

I am looking for someone with construction management experience to act as my Construction Advisor.

Is this something you might be interested in?

Explain the role of a Construction Advisor.
(See page 2)

interview 1 of 2

Instead of the financial and scheduling responsibilities of a general contractor, Construction Advisors have limited responsibilities and assist owners in managing their own projects by,

- *Reviewing blueprints,*
- *Reviewing subcontractor and supplier selections,*
- *Making site inspections,*
- *Consulting regularly with the owner on construction related matters.*

The job is a seven or eight month part time position, during which, Construction Advisors can work on other projects, as long as they can make regular building site inspections, take phone calls, and meet three times a month with the owner.

Construction Advisors assume no financial responsibilities, are not responsible for scheduling, and do not sign for permits.

Owners order materials select subcontractors and pay all bills.

Construction Advisors make regular building site inspections, interact with subcontractors and suppliers as needed, and advise the owners on a regular basis.

If the prospect is interested, discuss pay.
See part 2 of Construction/Construction Guides

Explain the status of the project, when construction will begin, and the approximate size of the home. Answer questions, offer to email a list of a Construction Advisor's responsibilities, and restrictions, See part 2 of construction/Construction Guides and suggest a meeting if the prospect seems acceptable and is interested.

Prospects email _____
      (See Construction Advisor responsibilities and restrictions in chapter 2)

Meet at _____
      (Building site, owners home, contractors office)

Date _____ Time _____
      (A suggested contract is located in Forms, Chapter11)

interview 2 of 2

LOCATING SUBCONTRACTORS

Calling Guides

You will need most or all of the sub-trades on the "Subcontractors Needed Checklist" to bid your project. List the ones you already know and check the ones you need to locate. Not all categories will apply to your project and you may be able to simplify by finding subs that offer multiple services.

If you make (get-acquainted) calls at a rate of six a day it should take only a few hours a day to assemble a complete list of *potential* subcontractors in less than a week. When finished, you will have a pool of specialists ready to bid and build your home. Keep your preliminary house plans in front of you as you make these calls. It will help you visualize what you are calling about and you will have details ready if a sub trade asks for them.

You are only calling to become acquainted. You will call back, to arrange meetings, provide plans and get formal bids. You are not asking potential sub trades to bid yet, but you should insure them that you have the property, that plans are almost finished, and you are securing or have financing.

Your pre-pricing efforts will be most productive if you shop for material suppliers and make initial contacts with potential sub trades at the same time.

Calling guides to locate subcontractors (initial contact)

Now is the time to start using your new project phone, your project address and your designated laptop so the people you contact don't clutter your home phone and show up on your doorstep uninvited. Your project files need to be ready to use before you start making these calls. Use the suggested file setup in this guide to organize your files and use a good accounting program to track finances. Load your phone with project numbers, notes and begin taking progress photos at the building site.

THESE ARE <u>PRE-PRICING</u> CALLS. KEEP IT SIMPLE
CALL SEVERAL OF EACH SUB CONTRACTOR TYPE
You will choose bidders and solicit bids later

Calling Scripts to Locate Subcontractors

See also Subcontractors needed checklist (TAB 5, page)

REFERENCES 3

Locate a Soils Engineer:

Soil testing is not usually required but, before issuing a building permit, some areas with expansive or soft soils require testing. Call your building department or check with your Construction Advisor. If a soils engineer is required, make the following call,

"Hello, my name is _____. I am planning to build a new home in the _____ area and understand I need a soils analysis in order to get a permit. Can you do the testing needed and can you give me an idea what it will cost and how long it will take?

Record the name number and date of your contact and details.

Locate a Surveyor / Civil Engineer

A plot plan is nearly always required with plans submission for a zoning permit and you may need a licensed surveyor to produce an accurate plot plan showing how your new home will fit on the lot and to locate buildings on adjacent properties.

It is also a good idea to employ a surveyor to stake out your house accurately for excavation and to set a correct grade for the dig. Many excavators do not test or adjust their survey instruments regularly and may not be careful in checking the house plans for any basement or footer depth requirements that vary from the norm. Of the many mistakes that can be made during construction, a mistake in depth or location during the initial dig or in squaring up the foundation footers or walls are the worst. If your house footprint has a complex shape or is on a lot with variable slopes, a surveyor is essential for the initial stake out.

Calling Guide
"Hello, my name is _____ and I am having a new home designed for a property at _____. I may need a survey and possibly a plot plan and an accurate house stake out. Do you provide these services for residential projects?" _____

"How do you charge for your services and what do I need to provide?"

_____

Record the name number and date of your contact and details

Locate a Brush and Tree Removal Service

Excavators can bulldoze small trees and brush out of the building area but leave you with a pile of rubbish and most are unwilling to haul it away. Tree removal companies, on the other hand use a large chipper and will leave you with a clean lot. Decide which trees need removed and have the stumps ground out. In general, any tree in the construction zone that will have its roots run over by heavy equipment probably won't survive.

Calling Guide
Hello, my name is _____ and I will be building a house in the _____ area soon. My lot has _____ that need to be removed before construction.

Do you provide those services? _____
Do you do stump grinding? _____

"Can I call you for an estimate when I'm ready?" _____

Record the name number and date of your contact and details.

Locate a Stump Grinding Service (if needed).

Calling Guide
"Hello, my name is _____ and I will be building a new home in the _____ area soon. I am having trees removed but will need stumps ground and removed. Do you provide these services? _____

"Can I call you for an estimate when I'm ready? _____

Record the name number and date of your contact and details.

Locate Potential Excavators

Not all excavators do residential work, preferring larger commercial projects, and not all excavators do the same things. Contact several excavating companies. A meeting at the building site will provide you with a wealth of information.

Calling Guide
"Hello my name is _____ and I will be building a house at _____ soon and will need an excavator to clear the lot and dig the foundation."

"Do you do residential work?" _____

"Do you also do septic systems?" _____

"Can you cut in my construction drive and bring in gravel" _____

"What about a culvert or curb cuts?" _____

"Can you connect to the water, sewer and gas taps and extend them to the house?"

_____

"Will you come back to backfill and give me a final dressed grade when the house is done?"

_____

This is one of your primary contractors ask his advice. His price will go down and his attention to detail will go up if you establish a relationship.

Record the name number and date of your contact and details.

Locate a Portable Toilet Supplier

Many locations require a portable bathroom be available on the construction site. You will need the portable facility for five or six months.

Calling Guide

"Hello My name is _____. I will be building a house in the _____ area soon and understand I will be required to have a portable potty available. Can you supply one for about five months and can you give me the cost?"

"Is there a deposit required?"

Record the name number and date of your contact and details.

Locate Potential Electricians

You need to engage your electrician early to acquire an electrical permit and to provide temporary electrical service to the construction site for use during construction. You may also need to set up an account with the local electric company. Ask your Construction Advisor about his preferences and call several companies. Keep in mind that other mechanical contractors, heating and plumbing, have to work around each other and around electrical wiring. A single company that does electrical, heating and plumbing can sometimes save money and avoid conflicts. These are primary contractors. Get acquainted, ask questions, and choose wisely. The electrician will be with you from start to finish.

Calling Guide

"Hello my name is _____ and I will be building a house at _____ and will need an electrician. Do you do residential work and will you be available in the near future?" _____

"I will need temporary service during construction. Can you set that up for me?" _____

"I will have working drawings for the house soon but no electrical plan. Can you give me an accurate bid if we go over the plans for special outlets and lights?" _____

"Does you company do other mechanical work like plumbing and heating?" _____ if not _____ Can you recommend a plumber or heating contractor?"

Record the name number and date of your contact and details.

Locate a Well Drilling Service (if needed)

If a well is required, an early call to the local health department is a good idea. They will have records of other wells in the area, depths, water quality, and names of drillers familiar with your area. If there is any doubt about finding water, you might want to pick a spot for the well and drill before construction starts.

Calling Guide
"Hello, my name is _____ and I will be building a house in the _____area in the near future. I will need a well. Do you drill wells in the area and can you give me any information on other wells in the area.

"Can I call you when I am ready?"

Record the name number and date of your contact and details.

Locate a Trash Dumpster Provider

You will need a dumpster to prevent a trash build up and to meet local requirements. It should be on site when your foundation work begins and its placement is important. It needs to be close enough to construction to be convenient but should not block access and should leave room for several pick-ups and for large lumber load deliveries. Organizing the construction site is important and before you actually have a dumpster delivered, a consultation with your project advisor is a good idea. For now, you are just getting information and establishing a contact.

Calling Guide
"Hello, my name is _____ and I will be building a house at
_____. Can you provide a dumpster during construction?" _____

_____

"What size do you recommend and what will you charge?" _____

"Do you charge for each pick up?" _____

Record the name number and date of your contact and details.

Locate Potential Foundation Installers

You must have decided on your foundation type. concrete block, poured concrete walls, superior wall etc.)

Calling Guide
"Hello, my name is _____, and I am going to build a new home in the _____ area soon. Do you service the area. _____ and do you install_____ (type of foundation)? _____

"Can you give me an accurate bid if I send you working drawings?
_____

"Can you include basement windows and other accessories?_____

"Can you visit the site in advance to be certain it meets your needs for access and materials deliveries? _____

Record the name number and date of your contact and details.

Locate Concrete Flat work Companies

You will need concrete floors poured at different times during your project. (basement, garage, driveway, patio, etc. Houses on slabs with no basement require the floor be in place before framing begins. A basement floor can be poured after framing is in place but, for certain types of precast foundation walls like Superior Walls, it must be poured before the dirt is backfilled around the foundation to prevent the bottom of the foundation walls from kicking in. Having framing weight on foundation walls also prevents the top of foundation walls from tipping in.

Calling Guide
"Hello my name is _____ and I will be building a new house in _____ soon. I will need basement and garage floors poured and later a driveway. Do you do residential work and do you provide the concrete? _____

Do you provide the gravel base?_____

Record the name number and date of your contact and details

Locate Potential Framing Crews

These companies may call themselves builders and usually prefer to arrange their own lumber deliveries to avoid delays and like to work with familiar contacts. A compromise may be required with you approving, and paying for lumber and window/ door orders. You need not discuss this now, but should ask which suppliers they usually work with. Also ask if they have framed any homes in the area and how many are on their crew.

Calling Guide
"Hello_____ my name is _____and I will be building a new house in _____ soon. Would your crew be interested in bidding to do the framing? Do you also do trim work?

Record the name number and date of your contact and details

Locate Roofing Companies

Not all roofing companies install all types of roofing materials. Very few work with slate roofs, and some may not work with shake or metal. Most work with shingles and simulated slate or shake and prefer to work with lighter materials, which may not be your selection. There are two basic types of roofing contractors, commercial and residential. Commercial contracting companies are usually larger and specialize in flat roofing techniques not in residential applications. Be as specific as you can about your project as you get acquainted with prospective roofers. Follow the same format as above. Keep detailed notes.

Locate Potential Siding Installers

You may need more than one sub contracting company to install siding if you are using more than one type of siding. For example wood lap siding or shake, vinyl siding, cultured stone or brick, or brick or stone veneer. These contractors usually advertise and except for a mason to lay true brick or stone can be located on line in the phone book or from your project advisor. Ask questions be excited about your project, set up meetings to view samples. Keep detailed records.

Locate Potential Plumbing Contractors

Like the electrician, you will need your plumbing contractor early in construction for an initial connection for construction water and for under slab lines. He will return to run lines through the walls and under frame floors and must pass an inspection for rough plumbing. Later he will connect all fixtures and must pass a final plumbing inspection. Tell him you would like to select all fixtures with his advice. Ask if he will be available and if he can supply the fixtures you select.

Locate Potential Heating and Cooling Contractors

Your selection here may be determined by the type of systems you plan on using to heat and cool. Be open to suggestions, ask questions and find out if they would like to bid. Do they install the type of heating you are considering, can they engineer the system?

Locate Potential Insulation Suppliers and Installers

As you talk to suppliers ask about types of insulation available and their advantages and disadvantages. Ask about venting through overhangs and eves just to see how attentive they are to this requirement. Ask about how long it will take and how they arrive at a forecast cost

You will select bids and select subcontractors later
See Tab 5, page for subcontractors needed checklist

REFERENCES 3

LOCATING CONSTRUCTION MATERIAL SUPPLIERS

CALLING GUIDES

You are calling to locate potential material suppliers for your project and to get information regarding their services. Try to establish a contact beyond the secretary. A salesperson or representative that becomes a trusted contact is essential when you need to place an order or have a question that requires an in depth knowledge of the products and services they offer.

The scripts do not cover all the suppliers you will need but should get you started. Use the calls to educate yourself and establish a rapport. Explain how you will be using a Project Advisor and will only begin construction when a construction loan is established. You may need to establish contacts and estimates in advance to finalize a loan.

Scripts Provided

    Locate Gravel and Stone Suppliers
    Locate Ready Mix Concrete Supplier
    Locate Brick and Decorate Stone Suppliers
    Locate Lumber Suppliers
    Locate Window and Sliding Glass Door Suppliers
    Locate Roofing material Suppliers
    Locate Other Needed Suppliers

See also, Construction Material Suppliers Needed (Tab 5, page)

Locate Gravel and Stone Suppliers If not provided by your excavator

Calling Guide
"Hello my name is _____ and I will be building a new house in _____ soon.

I will need gravel for a temporary driveway, for footer drains, the basement floor and more. Can you provide gravel for a residential project? _____

Can you spread gravel for drives etc? _____

Record the name number and date of your contact and details

NOTE: This contact can also provide prices you can use to evaluate labor and material quotes.

Locate Bulk Concrete Suppliers

Calling Guide
"Hello my name is _____ and I will be building a new house in _____ very soon.

I will need concrete for footers, basement and garage floors, and later a driveway. Do you provide concrete to residential projects?

_____

Can you advise me as to what mix to use? _____

Can you provide gravel? _____

If needed, can you provide gravel in a conc. truck if I need it chuted into a basement?

_____

Record the name number and date of your contact and details

NOTE: This contact can also provide prices you can use to evaluate labor and material quotes.

Locate Brick and Decorative Stone facing Suppliers

Decorative brick or stone facing for exterior walls, fireplace faces, and chimneys, etc. can be real brick and stone or cultured (artificial) brick or stone. Prices and labor are similar.

Cultured brick or stone is thin, is applied directly to almost any flat surface and is suitable for exterior and interior applications.

Real brick and stone has bulk size and if used as a skirt around the bottom of the house, (referred to as "brick or stone to grade") requires a ledge in the foundation wall that **must be shown on the foundation plan**. If your plans do not have a brick ledge shown on the foundation drawings, do not order real brick or stone.

Calling Guide
"Hello my name is _____ and I will be building a new house in _____ very soon.

I will need (real), (cultured)/(brick) or (stone). Can you provide this?_____

Do you have a show room? _____

Can you help me calculate how much I will need? _____

Record the name number and date of your contact and details

Locate Lumber Suppliers

A "carefully selected" large lumber company can become a primary supplier and can greatly simplify your material estimating and delivery scheduling efforts. A knowledgeable salesperson, assigned to your project, can also become a trusted advisor. A large lumber and materials supplier can often provide roofing materials, siding, windows and doors, interior trim materials, insulation and sometimes cabinetry.

Big box home-improvement stores may express an interest in your project and offer credit incentives, but they do not usually have the estimating expertise, material knowledge, or ordering and delivery capacity, to support a whole house project.

Calling Guide

"Hello my name is _____ and I will be building a new house in _____ very soon. I will need lumber, roofing materials. Windows and doors, siding, trim materials, etc. What materials can you supply?

Do you have a show room? _____

What window brands do you supply? _____

Can you calculate the materials I will need? _____

Will there be delivery charges? _____

Will I have a single helpful contact for the entire project? _____

> Note: The lumber supplier is your most important supplier. Become personally
> acquainted. Visit the company. Ask the salesperson or a representative
> to visit the building site to spot any delivery problems in advance.

Record the name number and date of your contact and details

Locate a Window and door Supplier if lumber company does not supply them.

Your blueprints should specify the brand, style, and sizes of skylights, windows, and sliding glass doors. If your lumber supplier does not regularly deal with the brands specified, you may need to call the manufacturer to locate a local distributer.

"Hello my name is _____ and I will be building a new house very soon in" _____

"Your windows are specified on my blueprints. Can you build a list from my prints, give me a price, and deliver them when the house is ready?" _____

"Can you advise me as to options, accessories and colors?" _____

"Do you have a show room?" _____

Record the name number and date of your contact and details

Locate a Roofing Materials Supplier

Shingles, shakes, and metal roofing, may be available through your lumber supplier but, if you need a specific product you may have to contact the manufacture to locate a supplier.

Calling Guide
Hello, I am building a new house in _____ and will need roofing materials in about _____ months

I am considering (type of roofing) _____

Can you suggest a supplier in my area? _____

I need to select colors etc. Does he have a show room? _____

Do you deliver (to the roof)? _____

Does the product require special application? _____

Is there a long lead-time for the product? _____

If I send you my blueprints, can you calculate the amount of roofing I will need? _____

Can you recommend a good roofing crew near where I will be building?

Record the name number and date of your contact and details

Note: See Tab 7 for instructions for calculating roofing materials needed.

Locate Other Needed Suppliers

Adapt previous calling guides as necessary to locate other construction material suppliers. Some materials may be available through home improvement stores. Use Home improvement stores primarily to make your preliminary personal selections

TAB 4

PROJECT FILES

The Importance of a Good Filing System

An effective paper filling system is essential for a successful custom home project.

Paper Files

    Legal
    Planning
    Construction Advisor
    Personal selections
    Subcontractors
    Material Suppliers
    Pricing Estimates / Quotes
    Projected Project Total Cost
    Construction Management
    Financial Management

Digital Files

The Importance of a Good Filing System

Accurate records are essential. For a full year you will be working with over fifty important new contacts, will be making almost one hundred selections and will be keeping the financial records for a large project. You will be inspecting, making decisions, organizing and overseeing an outdoor factory with a diverse array of assembly components and a constant turnover of specialized workers. The following suggested arrangement of files should be helpful. Set up your filing system early and keep it up to date. Even the mileage driven to meet with your designer and the dates and calls made to a supplier will become important records when you file taxes or need to solve a problem. Take photos and keep track of details. The time you spend at your desk keeping files current will net you thousands of dollars in savings and eliminate many hours spent recovering from an oversight.

To stay organized and make your supervisory responsibilities easy, you need a filing and record keeping system that matches the many planning and pricing steps involved and coincides with the labor and assembly steps required. A large box filled with plan books, magazines, realtors names, bank records, preliminary plans, labor bids, permits, lumber quotes, invoices due, and random photos, is not a filing system.

Projects managed without a good filing system are plagued with delays, failed inspections, price overruns, and mechanic's liens. The following suggested file arrangements should be helpful. Set up your filing system early and keep it up to date. Take photos and keep track of details.

Paper Files

Paper files require additional focus when making entries and an expanded perspective when being reviewed. Digital files are convenient and allow for quick entries and immediate retrievals. Both types of files are required for planning and managing a custom home project. Blueprints, contracts, material lists, proposals, and certain financial records require paper records for legal purposes and are effective visual presentations. They also provide storage and retrieval when an electronic device is not available.

An effective paper filling system is essential for a successful custom home project. Consider your paper files as you primary files and your digital files a supplement. Time spent keeping your paper files up to date keeps the project organized and forces you to think and stay ahead of scheduling requirements. Use your project phone and project lap top where appropriate but do not overlook or neglect a complete paper filing system. Things like documents, agreements, bids, bank records, invoices, inspections, and payments, are paper records that need filing.

(See suggested file organization below)

PROJECT FILES (suggested)

FILE Section1, Legal
> Loan agreements
> Real Estate
> Insurance
> Attorney
> Contracts
> Complaints
> Disputed Invoices / Payments

FILE Section 2, Design & Planning Management
> Design ideas file, (magazines, notes, sketches, photos, etc.)
> Prospective building site records (See part one of OCC)
> Selected building site pre-purchase records, (deed, owner,
> Survey/zoning, easements, utilities, building restrictions, etc)
> Special site requirements, (clearing, fill, grading, access)
> Designer/architect interviews / selection
> Design meetings and progress notes, (ideas, changes)
> Construction Advisor search and selection
> Approvals and Permits (well, septic, soils, zoning, building permit, utility connections,
>   access permits, curb cuts etc.)

FILE Section 3, Construction Advisor Acquisition / Management
> Contract and Compensation Agreement (see Forms, Tab 6)
> Required activities: inspections, meetings, calls (see part 2 of Planning)
> Call and text logs
> Site inspection logs
> Meeting records and notes
> Additional actions requested of Construction Advisor
> Delays / Problems

FILE Section 4, Personal Selections
> Selections needed checklist (copy from Tab 5)
> Personal selections deadlines (copy from Tab 5)
> Preliminary selections file
> Final selections file, contacts, details, price, lead times

Personal selections ordered / delivered
Delays / problems

FILE Section 5, Subcontractors

<u>Prospects</u>
Subcontractors needed checklist (copy from Tab 5)
Prospective subcontractor calling guides (copy from Tab 3)
Completed prospective subcontractor calls and notes
Prospective subcontractors list

<u>Solicited for bids</u>
Blank letter requesting bid (copy from Tab 6)
Bids solicited
Bids received

<u>Selected for work</u>
See subcontractors needed checklist (Tab 5)
Work progress reports / notes
Delays / problems

FILE Section 6, Material Suppliers

Suppliers needed checklist (copy from Tab 5)
Prospective supplier calling guides (copy from Tab 3)
Preliminary calls to material suppliers and notes

<u>Construction materials suppliers selected for bidding</u>
List of selected construction materials suppliers
Blueprints e-mailed
Bids received

<u>Construction materials suppliers contracted for work</u>
Material supplier contacts
Delivery details, loads, lead times, details. (See Tab 7 for loads)
Delays / problems

FILE Section 7, Pricing, Estimates / Quotes

Real estate fees, land costs, site improvement / site approval costs
Construction loan / other financial fees

Project insurance
Incidental management / oversight costs
   (supplies, equipment, phone, mileage, space, printing etc)
Project Advisor fees
Personal selections, (prices, quotes)
Subcontractor quotes, (labor only and labor and materials quotes)
Material supplier quotes, (add taxes and delivery)
Other estimates,
   (electricity to site, site cleanup, construction drive maintenance, inspection fees)

FILE Section 8, Projected Project Total Cost

<u>Building Site</u> and all related
<u>Legal, Construction Loan, Insurance</u> and all related
<u>Project Management and Oversight</u> and all related
<u>Project Advisor</u> and all related
<u>Owner selected items</u> and all related
<u>Labor only Cost</u> and all related
<u>Combined Labor and Material Costs</u> and all related
<u>Materials only Costs</u> and all related
<u>Other Project Costs</u> and all related
<u>Pricing Pad</u> and misc.

FILE Section 9, Construction Management

Copies of appropriate checklists from Tab 5
Copies of appropriate forms from Tab 6
Permits and approvals (issuance dates, copies, contact persons)
Progress records (daily logs, deliveries, work in progress)
     Project Advisor, building site inspection logs
     Owner, building site inspection logs
     Photo log and notes
     Phone log written notes
Inspections by Building Inspectors
Problems / delays and difficulties (encountered / solved)

FILE Section 10, Financial Management

Requires a detailed listing of all forecast project costs
<u>Keep a Construction Loan Bank Transactions and Statements File</u>

Establish Spreadsheet Listing all Forecast Project Expenses
Maintain a Current Invoice and Payments Due File
Maintain a Current Invoices and Expenses Paid File
Monitor Financial Progress:

Designate each spreadsheet entry as *Future, In Progress, or Complete*

Estimate *In Progress* entries as $ under or over on date with each payment

Calculate *Completed* entries for $ under or over with final payment

Compare over and under amounts to determine current Project Status

Subtract unexpected expenses from pricing pad until zero then as $ over

Digital Files

FILE Section 11, Digital Files

Keep Emergency and important contacts in project phone & laptop

Keep active subcontractors and suppliers in project phone & laptop

Scan important checklists and forms into laptop for printing copies

Use phone and laptop to back up paper *personal selections* files

Keep Construction Advisor info and record of all contacts in phone

Scan final construction drawings onto thumb drive and into laptop

Maintain a paper phone log of calls in and calls out, download daily
(See Tab 6)

Maintain photo logs with dates and notes in phones and laptop
Use owner's project phone and Construction Advisor's phone to
Photograph work in progress, deliveries, problems, etc.

Download and use an accounting program if desired but be aware,
few available programs can asses a construction project's interim
financial status. (See *Project Financial Management* above)

TAB 5

CHECKLISTS

BUILDING SITE EVALUATION CHECKLIST

Before you give a potential building site serious consideration or begin design work, give the following items consideration.

Set Back Requirement: minimum distance for house placement from the street right of way, (not the edge of pavement)

Side Yard Restrictions: minimum distance for house placement from side property lines

Room for Side Garage Entry: 30 feet is needed from the garage to a property line or any obstruction for a car to back out and turn. The garage is best set on the high side of the lot.

Does the Lot Dictate House Orientation? Consider; wind, sun, best views, and which side of the lot is higher. The garage is best placed on the high with the kitchen close to the garage

Topography: Consider sloping lot conditions, mounds or ravines, driveway slope, potential flooding and drainage.

Easements: Check for utility and other easements that will restrict access or house placement.

Driveway: Consider slope and any conflicts with underground or overhead utilities from the proposed house to the street. Are there concrete curbs at the street that will require cutting? Are there any obvious barriers or obstructions to a new driveway? Is a culvert needed?

Sewer Depths: Consider both sanitary and storm sewers. Is the sewer deep enough at the street for gravity flow from your proposed basement?

Sewer Taps: Are taps ready and on the property, if not, are the taps possible but will need cut into a main line, or are taps impossible or require main trunk extensions? Are there Tap fees? These could cost several thousand dollars.

BUILDING SITE EVALUATION CONTINUED

Septic System: If a septic system is required. Is a percolation test required? Has a required placement already been determined and is this compatible with the envisioned house placement?

Water: Is city water available? Is a tap in place? Will there be tap fees? If a well is needed what is the quality of the water?

Natural Gas: Is natural gas available? Is there a tap in place? Will there be tap fees?

Electricity: Is electricity immediately available overhead or underground? Will there be a line extension, hook up, or connection fee?

Noise: Visit the site at night. Is there excessive noise from freeways, airports etc.

Overhead: When you visit a potential building site, take the time to look up. Are there hillside houses looking down on the property? Are there power lines overhead or nearby?

Other Houses Are other houses in the neighborhood compatible with the house you envision.

Zoning Restrictions: Nearly all properties have zoning restrictions and you will need to get a zoning permit. Review these restrictions before you buy.

Restrictive Covenants/ Deed Restrictions: Developed areas may also have requirements, size limitations, exterior décor stipulations, etc. review these restrictions before you buy.

Homeowner Association Rules: Neighborhood regulatory bodies often establish color and style requirements.

Other Appurtenance Restrictions: Is there space for anticipated out buildings, pools, etc? Is fencing for pets allowed?

PRICING PERCENTAGES COMPARATIVE CHECKLIST

Typical material and labor components as a percentage of total building costs The following percentages are based on average cost for ten different projects in a size range of 2,200 square feet to 2,800 square feet. Each of the ten houses had individual square foot costs that varied greatly. Therefore, these figures as with any pricing generalization, must be used as a guide only. Trying to arrive at a total cost for a new home by pricing only one or a few of its components will be as inaccurate as trying to price by the square foot. There is only one way to arrive at a reasonably close forecast price for a new custom home and that is to go through the total bidding process of all materials, all labor, and all related costs and fees. There is no easy way other than to guess using partial information or to multiply size by a square foot guess, which equals a guess. The value of the following percentages is to show that any effort to keep costs under control requires attention to the cost of thirty or more elements, not just lumber and foundation. In general, it is not wise to concentrate cost cutting efforts on elements of the project that affect structural integrity.

Permits and tap fees	1½%
Lot improvements (tree removal, drive, utility-connections)	6%
Excavation and grading	2%
Trash receptacle and trash removal	1%
Foundation (labor and materials)	6%
Framing materials (roof, walls, floors)	8%
Framing labor (include window and exterior door installation)	7%
Roofing materials (felt, shingles, vents, etc.)	2%
Roofing labor -	1%
Windows, exterior doors, (garage doors installed) -	8½%
Siding, exterior trim (not brick or stone) -	2%
Siding labor -	1%
Plumbing materials and fixtures -	3½%
Plumbing labor -	3%
Heating and air conditioning materials -	2%
Heating and air conditioning labor -	2%
Electrical materials and lighting fixtures -	2½%
Electrical labor -	2 ½%
Insulation materials -	1 ½%

PRICING PERCENTAGES COMPARATIVE CONTINUED

Insulation labor -	1 ½%
Drywall materials -	1 ½%
Drywall labor -	2%
Interior doors, trim, stair materials -	4%
Trim labor -	3%
Cabinetry and counter tops (installed) -	8%
Paint and staining materials -	½%
Paint and staining labor -	2%
Floor coverings (installed) -	8%
Appliances (installed) -	3%
Knobs, misc. shelving	1%
Misc. materials	1%
Misc. labor	1%

SUB-TRADES NEEDED

Trades, **(in bold)** are the primary trades. Call these well in advance to ascertain availability. Make contact with all trades to establish an important contact list. Ask to talk to someone who can answer a few quick questions.

Soils Engineer, (if soils are in question or if engineering is required in your area)

Surveyor (lot survey – plot plan – house stake out – grade set)

Brush & Tree Removal
Stump Grinding (if separate from above)

Excavator 1 (remove top soil – dig foundation – install temporary drive – backfill – misc.)

Excavator 2 (if required to connect water & sewer or septic)

Porto Potty (an outdoor toilet may be required for your project)

Electrician (to obtain permit and provide temporary service to Building site after lot is cleared)

Well drilling (if required)

Dumpster

Mason for foundation or precast foundation supplier.

Concrete flat work crew

Clean up labor (ongoing to back up subs)

Shell erection crew 1, (rough carpentry crew)

Shell erection crew 2, (to erect specialty items or materials)

Roofing crew

Siding/ exterior trim crew

Gutter & downspout installer

SUB TRADES NEEDED CONTINUED

Plumber

Heating and Air Conditioning contractor

Other mechanical systems 1 (Security, TV Audio, Vacuum)

Insulation installer

Drywall crew

Painting / Staining crew

Cabinetry & counter top installer

Interior trim crew (install interior doors & trim)
Specialty stair & railing installer (if required)
Specialty trim or built-in trim crew (if required)

Door knob installation laborer

Flooring installation (type 1)
Flooring installation (type 2)
Flooring installation (type 3)

Appliance installation

Light fixture installation, (electrician or supplier)

Driveway crew (concrete / asphalt if separate)

Sidewalk installation crew (if separate)

Landscaping crew

CONSTRUCTION MATERIAL SUPPLIERS NEEDED

You will need most or all of the following suppliers to bid your project. List the ones you already know and check the ones you still need to locate. Not all categories will apply to your project.

Dumpster rental / construction trash disposal
Portable toilet rental
Gravel supplier for (foundation, temporary drive, trenches)
Concrete ready mix supplier
Concrete Block supplier
Specialty foundation systems (superior wall, poured concrete, other)
Lumber / trim & interior door supplier
Specialty shell materials supplier #1, insulated panels etc. if specified
Specialty shell materials supplier #2, roof trusses/ floor trusses etc
     (if not available from lumber supplier)
Specialty shell materials supplier #3, beams & columns,
     (if not available from lumber supplier)
Specialty shell materials supplier #4, (other specialty materials)
Windows/ Sliding glass/ French-door supplier (if not lumber supplier)
Exterior door supplier, formal entry doors (if not lumber supplier)
Roofing materials supplier
Siding material supplier type #1
Siding material supplier type #2
Plumbing fixture supplier
Bath & kitchen accessories supplier
Cabinetry supplier
Counter top supplier
Garage door supplier – installer
Insulation supplier – installer
Drywall supplier – installer
Paint supplier – applicator
Finished floor type 1 supplier – installer
Finished floor type 2 supplier – installer
Finished floor type 3 supplier – installer
Lighting fixture supplier – installer
Closet accessory supplier – installer
Appliance supplier

ITEMS REQUIRING SELECTION BY THE OWNER

During the design process, you can get ahead of the game by making pre-selections for price. These selections will need finalized as construction progresses but by making preliminary selections you will arrive at a more accurate forecast project cost and avoid construction delays. (See selections deadline checklist. (This Tab). Following is a partial list of selection items you may want to select for style, color, manufacture, etc. Make a list of your pre-selections, their price, location, manufacture, etc. You are not making final selections, only selections needed to arrive at an accurate price when your final house plans are ready.

Pre-Select in the order needed for construction. (See selections deadline checklist).

Exterior brick and stone (may affect foundation drawings)
Supplier, type, color or name, coverage, price _____
_____

Intercom, security, automated systems, built-in vacuum
Installed _____

_____

Residential elevator (will affect design drawings)
Supplier, type, details, price, installed_____
_____

Plumbing fixtures
Suppliers, manufacturers, style, color, finish, price _____

_____

Toilets	Disposal
Tubs, Showers	Sump Pump
Faucets, Shower heads	Appliance Hookups

ITEMS REQUIRING SELECTION BY OWNER CONTINUED

Temporary exterior man doors and locksets
(doors that could be damaged during construction)

Used, size, type, locksets, multiple keys, supplier, price

Permanent exterior man doors and locksets

New, type, size, hand, style, locksets, supplier, color, price

---

Garage doors

Type, width, height, style, color, windows, installed price,

Interior doors

Type, size, pre-hung, style, wood, composite, price

Roofing materials

Type (asphalt, metal, slate, shake), color, coverage, price

Appliances

Supplier, model, color, features, size, price, installed

Range,	Ovens	Dishwasher
Cook-top,	Refrigerator	Wine cooler
Range top vent	Freezer	Washer / Dryer

Cabinetry

Style, wood species, color, assembled, installed price/ per foot

| Kitchen | Laundry | Medicine Cabinets |
| Baths | Library / Study | Cabinet Knobs |

ITEMS REQUIRING SELECTION BY OWNER CONTINUED

Counter tops
Material, style, special features, price per foot/ sq ft.

_____

Kitchen   Laundry   Baths   Bar

Exterior siding material
Type, coverage, color, installed price _____

_____

Shake   Vinyl   Stucco   Trim
Wood   Paint   Stain

Electrical
Switch types, outlet covers, color _____

_____

Fireplace Details
Gas inserts, doors or screen, mantle, tools, price _____

_____

Special ceiling materials
Type, style, coverage, color, price

_____

Wood   Drop   Soft Tile
Metal   Plaster   Beamed Other

Interior trim materials
Type, profile, wood species or composite, size, price/ linear ft

_____

Crown molding Wainscot Casing Baseboard
Railings, stair parts, risers and treads (oak, pine)

ITEMS REQUIRING SELECTION BY OWNER CONTINUED

Floor coverings

By room, type, description, supplier, color, installed, price

---

Lighting fixtures

Type, room, description, supplier, installed, price

Closet materials

Details, design company, installed, price

Shower and tub doors

Size, style, supplier, model number, price

Mirrors

Plate glass, framed, size, location

OWNER SELECTIONS DEADLINES

If you have made a concerted effort in making preliminary selections for price to forecast the cost of your project and in making final selections to order materials and have them arrive on site when needed, things will go smoothly. Use construction progress to set your final selections deadlines. *For example*, if the project is in the excavation phase, you should be finalizing your plumbing fixture selections and selecting a kitchen designer.

Preparation Phase —
Exterior brick and stone selections due, don't forget mortar color.

Excavation Phase
Plumbing fixture selections due, especially tub and shower units too large to fit through doors and must be delivered as walls go up.
Final kitchen designer selected. (Cabinetry and counter top selections due later).

Foundation Phase
Roofing selections due (metal/ shake/ shingles, color and style).
Intercom/ built in entertainment/ security/ other electronic systems selections due.
Exterior and interior doorknob selections due

Shell Erection Phase
Cabinetry and counter top selections due. (May have a long lead time)
Built in medicine cabinet selections due, (framing carpenters need sizes).
Exterior siding and trim selections due
Floor plans marked-up with special electrical needs due,
(The electrician needs information prior to a walk through)

Basement Floor Concrete Pouring Phase
Appliance selections due, (needed by kitchen designer)
Exterior door selections (with lockset selections) due (refer to blueprints)
Garage door selections due

OWNER SELECTIONS DEADLINES CONTINUED

Roofing Phase
Walk through with electrician due, (final choices for wiring and light locations).
Interior door styles and trim selections due
Pre-built stair selections due (if any)

Exterior Finish Phase
Wood ceilings/ paneling styles and color selections due.

Electrical Phase
Fireplace-face detail selections due, especially if manufactured units are used.

Plumbing Phase
Floor covering selections due
Basement finish options selected.
Exterior deck and patio design selections due

Heating and cooling phase
Lighting Fixture selections due

Insulation Phase
Special trim items selections due.
Special closet items selections due.
Interior trim paint and stain color selections due.

Drywall Phase
Miscellaneous bath items selections due. Towel bars, toilet paper
holders, grab bars, etc
Plate glass mirror selections due.
Final furnace options selection due

TAB 6

FORMS

CONSTRUCTION ADVISOR AGREEMENT

Agreement Between:

Name_____, hereinafter known as
The Owner/s

and:

Name: _____, herein after known as
The Construction Advisor

Purpose of the Agreement:

To establish a working relationship between The Owner/s, endeavoring to plan and build a custom home, and a Construction Advisor engaged as an advisor on construction related matters.

To specify and limit the agreement to the specific construction project being undertaken by the owner/s, herein after known as *The Project*

To specify the terms of the agreement

To specify the responsibilities of both parties to the agreement

To specify the employed status of the Construction Advisor

To specify compensations for advisory services provided by The Construction Advisor

Limitations of the Agreement

Terms and responsibilities related to this agreement are limited to a new custom home project known as_____ to be constructed at _____,
with actual construction to begin on or about _____

Agreement Page 1 of 5

CONSTRUCTION ADVISOR AGREEMENT CONTINUED

<u>Terms of the Agreement</u>

This agreement is established to fulfill the owner/s' need for advice in the planning and construction of a new home. The position is to be temporary and part-time with an approximate duration of eight months.

Both parties will meet their responsibilities as specified herein. Any *substantial* transfer, increase, or decrease of responsibilities will require a modification of this agreement signed by both parties.

Both parties to this agreement may terminate the agreement in writing without cause but must provide a reasonable advanced notice of intent to terminate the agreement of not less than two weeks.

At / or near, the end of 'The Project', and at the sole determination of the Owner/s, the advisory services of the Construction Advisor can be terminated by formal written notification and a final payment of any compensation due for advisory services rendered.

<u>Responsibilities under The Agreement</u>

Responsibilities of the Owner/s

The Owner/s is/are responsible for the overall project including The Projects financing, planning, design, and construction. Owners are responsible for locating and selecting a building site, employing an architect/designer, locating and contracting with all sub trades and suppliers, and in selecting a Construction Advisor to assist in the oversight of construction.

The Owner/s will make all final decisions regarding the design and construction of the custom home referred to as 'The Project', and will schedule all work, all deliveries, and pay all bills.

Agreement Page 2 of 5

CONSTRUCTION ADVISOR AGREEMENT CONTINUED

Responsibilities of the Construction Advisor

During the Planning Phase of The Project, Construction Advisors will assist the owner in reading blueprints, evaluating prospective subcontractors, evaluating material suppliers, and by providing guidance for obtaining permits. Construction Advisors will assist owners in locating specialty tradesmen, sources for unusual or hard to find materials, and in solving complex problems.

During the Construction Phase of The Project, Construction Advisors will establish early rapport with selected subcontractors and suppliers and explain the role of the Owner/s as the project manager and the Construction Advisor's role as advisor to the owner as a quality control inspector.

Construction Advisors will be reasonably available for phone consultations and will meet with the owner at least three times per month during regularly scheduled Construction Advisor building site inspections, or at another location.

Construction Advisor responsibilities include meetings, inspections, consultations, and three building site visits per week to inspect work-in-progress. Using their own cell phone, they are required to take photographs of work in progress and deliveries, to note materials needed, and correct any sub standard work. After each site inspection, the Construction Advisor forwards photos and any observations, problems, and suggestions, via text, to the owner's project phone. Any serious conditions or situations require a verbal notification.

Construction Advisors will provide their own transportation and travel as needed within their local area to meet with the owners, make building site inspections and meet other reasonable requests to travel locally in support of The Project. To keep accounting simple a mileage allowance is included in monthly payments for advisory services.

Agreement Page 3 of 5

REFERENCES 6

CONSTRUCTION ADVISOR AGREEMENT CONTINUED

Responsibilities of the Construction Advisor Continued

Construction Advisors will talk to subcontractors and suppliers on a regular basis to asses the status of the project, become aware of any problems or needed supplies, pass on or clarify the owner's instructions, and arbitrate misunderstandings on request. Construction Advisors will help resolve problems without usurping the owner's authority.

Construction Advisors will take and forward construction site photographs, and text, site visit comments to the Owner/s immediately after each site visit. Construction Advisors will complete and submit a photo and a text or e-mail site inspection report the same day of each site inspection.

Construction Advisors will make three building site inspections per week.

Construction Advisors will consult with the Owner/s twice per week by phone.

Construction Advisors will meet personally with the Owner/s three times per month.

Employment Status of The Construction Advisor

Construction Advisors are retained as part time 1099 advisors with no scheduling, purchasing or financing responsibilities. Construction Advisors are retained month-to-month for professional advice, building site inspections, consultations, and other advisory duties.

Construction Advisors are encouraged to continue or accept other work that does not conflict with their part time responsibilities under this agreement, but must disclose immediately, other obligations that make it difficult or impossible to meet the obligations specified by this agreement.

Agreement Page 4 of 5

CONSTRUCTION ADVISOR AGREEMENT CONTINUED

Construction Advisor Compensation
(see Part 2 of Design / Planning for suggested compensation)

The Construction Advisor will be retained on a month-to-month basis and compensated for part time services at a rate of $ _____ per month, during the final two months of the planning phase and at a rate of $_____ per month, during the seven-month construction phase. Retained service compensation is to be paid *in advance* for each month the Construction Advisor is retained.

Additional compensation

- Approved additional construction site inspections with reports, (three per week are required by contract), $_____ per additional visit.
- $_____ per additional meeting with the owner or others requested or approved by the owner, (three per month are required by contract). (not to include unplanned casual meetings)
- $_____ per additional telephone consultation or conference calls initiated by the owner, (two per week are required by contract).
- The Owner will compensate the Construction Advisor for additional site inspections, phone consultations, and meetings, requested by the Owner/s, in the Construction Advisor's next monthly retainer.

Construction Advisor compensation will begin with the signing of this agreement and continue as long as the Construction Advisor is retained. The issuance of a building permit will mark the end of the planning phase and the beginning of the construction phase. The issuance of an occupancy permit will mark the end of the project.

Owner/s _____ Date _____

Construction Advisor _____ Date _____

Agreement Page 5 of 5

REQUEST FOR WRITTEN BID
FROM SUBCONTRACTOR

Residential contracting is very different from the formal arrangements required in larger commercial projects. Many residential contractors are mom and pop operations using simple contracts and handshakes to consummate agreements.

Introducing detailed contracts and unfamiliar formal agreements into the residential bidding process can intimidate and eliminate good potential subcontractors or cause them to pad their bids to cover possible legal expenses. Most subcontractors have bid forms they use regularly and are comfortable with. Most are suitable as a contract or as the basis for a contract. Residential bids fall short in providing details, especially an approximate time to complete the work and the size of the crew they will use. These missing details prevent the Owner from evaluating the reasonableness, of both labor only bids and labor and material bids.

One way to encourage bidders to provide additional information, without introducing scary looking legal documents, is to include a request for estimates for "time to complete" and "the size of the crew they will use." as a letter accompanying a request for bid.

Sample Request for Bid

From _____Owner_____ Date_____

To _____

Please use the accompanying blueprints to prepare a proposal for labor or labor and materials and return your quote promptly. I anticipate obtaining loan approval and building permits soon with work beginning immediately thereafter.

To accommodate my construction lender please include with your bid, along with a description of the work, the anticipated time needed to complete your phase of the work and the size of the crew you will provide,

Include details on materials you will provide and details on any special, connectors, or equipment required.

OWNER PHONE CALL LOGS

Copy all calls from Project Phone before erasing
Log all calls **I** incoming **O** outgoing

Date_____ I / O _____ To/ From _____

Subject_____

Date_____ I / O _____ To/ From _____

Subject_____

Date_____ I / O _____ To/ From _____

Subject_____

Date_____ I / O _____ To/ From _____

Subject_____

Date_____ I / O _____ To/ From _____

Subject_____

Date_____ I / O _____ To/ From _____

Subject_____

Date_____ I / O _____ To/ From _____

Subject_____

MATERIALS ORDERED/DELIVERED LOG

O ordered **D** delivered

Date____ O / D ____ Supplier _____

Type Materials_____

Notes (due date) (damage) (missing) _____

Date____ O / D ____ Supplier _____

Type Materials_____

Notes (due date) (damage) (missing) _____

Date____ O / D ____ Supplier _____

Type Materials_____

Notes (due date) (damage) (missing) _____

Date____ O / D ____ Supplier _____

Type Materials_____

Notes (due date) (damage) (missing) _____

Date____ O / D ____ Supplier _____

Type Materials_____

Notes (due date) (damage) (missing) _____

DELAYS AND PROBLEMS LOG

*Date _____Brought to attention of _____

By _____

Delay or Problem _____

Follow up needed _____

*Date _____Brought to attention of _____

By _____

Delay or Problem _____

Follow up needed _____

*Date _____Brought to attention of _____

By _____

Delay or Problem _____

Follow up needed _____

*Date _____Brought to attention of _____

By _____

Delay or Problem _____

Follow up needed _____

CHANGE SUGGESTION AND AGREEMENT

Best if filled out by individual suggesting the change

DATE _____

SUGGESTED BY _____

DESCRIPTION OF CHANGE

_____

_____

_____

Reviewed by Owner Date _____ Initials _____

Reviewed by Construction Advisor Date _____ Initials _____

Reviewed by Designer/Architect Date _____ Initials _____

Reviewed by Affected Subcontractors

Name _____ Date _____ Initials _____

Name _____ Date _____ Initials _____

Reviewed by Affected Suppliers

Name _____ Date _____ Initials _____

Approved / Disapproved Date _____
Owner's signature _____

Final Change Description and Details _____

_____

_____

RECORD OF CONSTRUCTION ADVISOR

SITE VISIT

Take photos and forward with report to owner. Follow up with text to insure receipt.

DATE _____ TIME _____

WEATHER _____

Subcontractors working TYPE _____

NUMBER ON CREW _____

_____

     SUBCONTRACTOR   COMMENTS REQUESTS   COMPLAINTS

Subcontractors scheduled but missing _____

REASON _____

Subcontractors needed next _____

Work in progress _____
          STATUS   EXAMPLE (First Floor Walls Up)

Inspections made / passed? _____

Site conditions _____
       SAFETY   CLUTTER   DRIVEWAY CONDITION

_____

     MATERIALS   PROTECTED?   ACCESSIBLE (For Cranes Etc.)

Materials Delivered _____

Materials Needed _____

Owner selected items needed _____

Comments, Problems, Delays _____

RECORD OF OWNER

SITE VISIT

Take photos and transfer with report to permanent files, compare to Const Advisor report

DATE _____ TIME _____

WEATHER _____

Subcontractors working _____
                            TYPES   NUMBER ON CREW

_____

   SUBCONTRACTOR COMMENTS   REQUESTS   COMPLAINTS

_____

Subcontractors scheduled but missing _____
                                        REASON

Subcontractors needed next _____

Work in progress _____
                 STATUS   EXAMPLE (First Floor Walls Up)

Site conditions _____
            SAFETY   CLUTTER   DRIVEWAY CONDITION

_____

   MATERIALS ON SITE   MISSING   PROTECTED?

Materials Delivered _____

Materials Needed _____

Owner selected items needed _____

Comments_____

Attitudes, Problems, Delays

_____

_____

SITE ACQUISITION EXPENSES

Travel Expenses

Date _____ Description _____ Amount $ _____

Date _____ Description _____ Amount $ _____

Date _____ Description _____ Amount $ _____

Date _____ Description _____ Amount $ _____

Date _____ Description _____ Amount $ _____

Real Estate Fees/ Commissions

Date _____ Description _____ Amount $ _____

Contact Information: Name_____

Phone 1_____ Phone 2_____

Company_____ Address_____

Miscellaneous site acquisition expenses

Date _____ Description _____ Amount $ _____

Contact Information: Name _____Phone 1_____

Address_____

Notes _____

Site acquisition expenses 1 of 2

SITE ACQUISITION EXPENSES CONTINUED

Lot/ Land Costs

Date _____ Description
_____ Amount $ _____
Contact Information: Name _____Phone 1_____
Company_____ Address_____
Notes _____

Date _____ Description
_____ Amount $ _____
Contact Information: Name _____Phone 1_____
Company_____ Address_____
Notes _____

Other Site acquisition Costs, (test drilling, soils engineers, survey etc.)

Date _____ Description
_____ Amount $ _____
Contact Information: Name _____Phone 1_____
Company_____ Address_____
Notes _____

Date _____ Description
_____ Amount $ _____
Contact Information: Name _____Phone 1_____
Company_____ Address_____
Notes _____

TOTAL SITE ACQUISITION EXPENSES $ _____

Site acquisition expenses Page 2 of 2

ARCHITECTURAL DESIGN EXPENSES

Purchased Plans

Date _____ Description _____ Amount $ _____

Date _____ Description _____ Amount $ _____

Date _____ Description _____ Amount $ _____

Books/ Magazines

Date _____ Description _____ Amount $ _____

Date _____ Description _____ Amount $ _____

Date _____ Description _____ Amount $ _____

Date _____ Description _____ Amount $ _____

Date _____ Description _____ Amount $ _____

Date _____ Description _____ Amount $ _____

Computer Home Design Programs

Date _____ Description _____ Amount $ _____

Date _____ Description _____ Amount $ _____

Consultations/ Seminars

Date _____ Description _____

Mileage _____ Cost _____

Contact Information: Name _____ Phone _____

Company _____ Address _____

Notes _____

Design expenses Page 1 of 2

ARCHITECTURAL DESIGN EXPENSES CONTINUED

Lot improvement Plan / Survey

Date _____ Company_____ Cost $ _____

Contact Information: Name _____ Phone _____

Address _____

Notes _____

Design Engineering (shear wall compliance, beams, loads etc)

Date _____ Company_____ Cost $ _____

Contact Information: Name _____ Phone _____

Address _____

Notes _____

Architectural Design/ Drafting Fees

Date _____ Company_____ Cost $ _____

Contact Information: Name _____ Phone _____

Address _____

Notes _____

Incidental Design Costs, (mileage, printing, digital devices etc)

_____

_____

_____

TOTAL DESIGN EXPENSES $ _____

TAB 7

MATERIAL QUANTITIES AND BIDS

Lumber companies employ individuals that are adept at using blueprints to calculate the sheets of plywood, bundles of shingles, and number of 2x4s needed to build a new home. Creating a material list is time consuming and expensive to produce; they are therefore considered proprietary information. As a result, when you ask for a construction materials bid you get a package price, not a list with individual prices. On larger homes and additions, the best you can do is to ask the materials supplier to break the overall lumber package into truckloads and to price the loads separately.

Examples of lumber loads are:

- Basement support walls/ First Floor deck framing materials
- First Floor walls (exterior and interior wall materials)
- Second Floor deck framing materials
- Second Floor walls (exterior and interior wall materials)
- Roof Trusses (the price for truss packages is normally only disclosed to companies making repetitive purchases).
- Roof Framing materials

You can locate individual prices on-line and at Big Box home improvement stores and they may offer attractive payment plans for quantity purchases, but use caution. Big Box retailers are oriented toward small *off-the-shelf* purchases. They contract with outside companies to do material takeoffs from blueprints, and limit material offered to materials in their inventory or those available through established suppliers. Big Box stores are not equipped to store large loads inside or to deliver loads that won't fit on store trucks. They also cannot deliver to upper floors or rooftops. Big Box stores are, however, a good source for making and pricing preliminary personal selections.

Knowing the amounts and prices of all the materials needed lets you to evaluate bulk prices by isolating markups and labor costs. The process is time consuming and requires numerous repetitive measurements and calculations but becomes less intimidating if you concentrate on, *labor-and-material-bids*, *installation-included-bids*, and *material-only-bids*.

Concentrate on bids that include materials you can identify, count, and price. It also helps to realize that you are calculating *comparative estimates*, not trying to determine exact amounts or prices.

Labor and material bids:
(These bids are labor intensive and susceptible to excessive overhead estimates. Material quantities in starred items, can be estimated as a way to spot overpricing)

- Excavator utility connections to street, drive cuts and gravel
- Well or septic system
- *Concrete flat work, (slab floors, basement floors, driveways)
- Basement walls, (block, poured concrete)
- *Roofing, when materials are supplied by installer
- *Siding, when materials are supplied by installer
- *Insulation
- *Drywall

Bids that include important owner selections:

- *Brick and stone facing
- *Electrical, (switch types, plates, and color) if supplied by installer
- *Plumbing, (fixture brand, style, and color) if supplied by installer
- Heating and cooling, (brand, type, and features) if by installer
- *Roofing materials
- *Siding materials
- Landscaping

Bids priced as "installation included"

- Superior Wall basements
- *Appliances
- *Large lighting fixtures
- *Floor coverings
- Security and other automated systems

Material only bids:
(These bids are susceptible to excessive markups. Material prices in starred items, can be estimated)

- *Lumber, moldings, and other trim materials
- Trusses and other engineered products
- *Windows and sliding glass doors
- *Exterior entry doors
- *Interior doors
- *Door locksets and knobs
- *Cabinetry knobs and accessories

Labor only bids:
(These bids are susceptible to excessive labor and overhead markups. Material and overhead prices in starred items, can be estimated if the bid includes size of crew and days to complete)

- Lot survey, grade set, house stakeout, plot plan
- Excavation (dig, clearing, and grading)
- *Framing labor
- *Roofing labor (if materials supplied by owner)
- *Trim labor
- Special needs labor, (clean up, touch up, special installs)
- Door and cabinet knob installation

To determine if a bid is reasonable, it is necessary to estimate either the cost of the materials quoted or the man-hours involved. With material quantities and costs separated or labor, overhead, and handling charges estimated, excessive overhead or markups become evident.

If the bidder has responded to the *Bid Request Letter*, (*see Tab 6, Forms*). With the size of the crew and the number of days needed to complete the work, you can calculate man-hours, estimate reasonable labor costs, and guess at overhead and handling charges. If you are within 20% of the bid it is probably within your margin of error and not worth haggling over but, if the exposed labor portion is double or triple what you estimated, the bid needs a second look.

If you decide to do material quantity takeoffs from your blueprints, take quick measurements and use a hand calculator to keep track of running totals. Label and write results on a scratch pad leaving room to write prices and totals. Round off to the nearest foot, avoid large errors but don't worry about small ones, you are *estimating*.

The process is a simple five-step process.

1. Use the blueprints to measure and list key lengths, *basement outside wall lengths, and frame exterior and interior wall lengths.*
2. Use exterior wall measurements to calculate a few square footages.
3. Refer to the blueprints to determine the type of material specified
4. Using a few simple formulae turn your measurements into material quantities.
5. Find individual prices on line or in stores then multiply by the quantities calculated to determine total material costs.

Step One – Establish Key Linier Footages

Key linear measurements are essential for construction material estimating. Linier measurements are simply the length, *in feet*, of a wall or the length, *in feet*, of the side of a roof or a concrete slab etc.

Determine key linier footage amounts by measuring distances on the blueprints. Measuring is much faster than looking for dimensions. Remember, you are estimating and don't need to be exact. Record measurements to nearest even feet; disregard inches. Do not use a ruler. Most blueprints use a ¼" scale, *1/4" = 1 foot* and, If you use a ruler and measure 31/2", you have to multiply by four to get the number of feet. To avoid doing several hundred, multiplications in your head, and making mistakes, buy a cheep triangular architects scale from an office supply store. Find the side with ¼" and note that it has numbers of feet going up from the ¼" end and numbers coming from the other end at a different scale. Use the increasing ¼" (foot) numbers and note that at the ¼" end there are little marks. These are inch marks. You don't need them for materials estimating. Put a small piece of tape over the inch marks. The tape will keep you from measuring from the wrong place on the scale, and will help you find the side and the end of the triangular scale you need.

Measure quickly and write down every measurement. Measure to the nearest foot; don't worry about small mistakes, they will balance out. Use a hand calculator to determine a total for each key linier footage amount. *Label and record the totals.* You will use them repeatedly to establish many material quantities.

Record key linear feet
    (1) Measure the outside length of basement masonry walls.
    (2) Measure basement exterior *frame* walls, if any
    (3) Measure basement interior *frame* walls, if any
    (4) Measure first floor walls, exterior then interior
    (5) Measure second floor walls, exterior then interior

NOTE:
- Measure exterior walls first, (list totals separately).
- Measure interior walls next, (list totals separately).
- Measure walls from corner to corner.
- Don't try to be exact, nearest next foot is good enough, (over estimates are better than under estimates).

- **When measuring wall lengths ignore wall openings,** *(measure across them as if they weren't there)*
- If walls vary in height, (some are eight feet high and some nine feet high), measure and list them separately.
- Measure and record window and door opening widths in basement **exterior** walls, then first-floor exterior walls, then second-floor exterior walls. Don't waste time trying to be exact. Window and door headers overlap openings by 4". Overestimate for overlap and scrap
- Measure and record door and passageway openings for basement **Interior** frame walls, then first floor interior walls, then second floor interior walls. Overestimate

Note: Openings over eight feet may require an engineered header. These headers are noted as "LVLs" on the blueprints. List them separately.

Your list of key linier feet should include

Basement exterior <u>frame walls</u> *if any*, linear ft _____
Basement interior <u>frame walls</u> *if any*, linear ft._____

First Floor 8' high <u>exterior</u> frame walls, linear ft._____
First Floor 9' high <u>exterior</u> frame walls, linear ft._____
First Floor 10' high <u>exterior</u> frame walls, linear ft._____

First Floor 8' <u>interior</u> frame walls, linier feet _____
First Floor 9' <u>interior</u> frame walls, linier feet _____
First Floor 10' <u>interior</u> frame walls, linier feet _____

Second Floor 8' <u>exterior</u> frame walls, linear ft._____
Second Floor 9' <u>exterior</u> frame walls, linear ft._____
Second Floor 10' <u>exterior</u> frame walls, linear ft._____

Second Floor 8' <u>interior</u> frame walls, linier ft. _____
Second Floor 9' <u>interior</u> frame walls, linier ft. _____
Second Floor 10' <u>interior</u> frame walls, linier ft. _____

Other Frame Walls, <u>interior</u> linear ft._____
Other Frame Walls, <u>exterior</u> linear ft._____

Wall Openings, Linier Feet

Basement exterior wall opening widths, total linear ft. _____
Basement Interior frame wall openings, total linier ft. _____
First Floor exterior wall opening widths, total linear ft. _____
First Floor interior wall opening widths, total linier ft. _____
Second Floor exterior wall opening widths, total linear ft. _____
Second Floor Interior wall openings, total linear ft. _____

Step Two – Establish Key Square Footage Amounts

Square footage is simply the length of a rectangle multiplied by its width. Break up the foundation, first floor, and second floor into as many rectangles, squares, or triangles as needed, determine the square footage of each and add them together to determine each floor's square footage. Many combined labor and materials bids are of the square footage type.

Computing square feet is easy if the house is rectangular. Simply multiply width by length. If the shape of the house is more complex, divide the shape into rectangles and triangles, determine the square feet of each and add them together. Triangles are ½ of a square or a rectangle. Accuracy is important but don't waste time trying to be exact.

Copy the *exterior* wall dimensions from above starting with the basement. Calculate and record the square footage of the basement / crawl space / slab. Then calculate separate square footages for the garage, porches, etc. Calculate the square footage of the first and second floor in the same way.

Your list of key square feet should include the following,

Basement crawl space or slab square feet _____
Garage square feet _____
Porch square feet _____
First-Floor square feet _____
Second-Floor square feet _____

Roof square footages are a bit harder. Measure on elevation drawings, (front, side or rear views). Determine the width of the roof by measuring along the side with rain gutters. Determine the slope-distance by measuring along the angled line of the roof on a side view. Include the roof overhang. Multiply the gutter-distance by the slope-distance to determine the square footage of each portion of the roof. If the roof is complex, break it into squares and triangles. Again, don't try to be exact.

The above works well for gable roofs, but does not work for hip roofs. To calculate the square footage of a hip roof, determine the roof's **flat square footage**, (similar to computing the square footage of the floor area directly under the roof but, (add overhangs). The slope of a roof is, *by convention*, annotated as the number of feet of rise in 12 feet of run. For example, if a roof rises five vertical feet for every twelve horizontal feet, it has a slope of 5/12. You can find the slope listed on the blueprints.

To determine the square footage of a hip roof, multiply the roof's *Flat* square footage, *including the overhangs*, by the *Slope Factor* below.

"SLOPE"	"SLOPE FACTOR"	
4/12	- 1.05	
5/12	- 1.08	
6/12	- 1.12	
8/12	- 1.20	------- steepest a man can stand on
10/12	- 1.30	
12/12	- 1.41	------ 45 degrees
14/12	- 1.54	

Example, for an 8/12 hip roof, 3,400 sq ft flat X 1.20 slope factor = 4,080 actual sq ft.

Key square footages determine the following materials

To determine gravel and concrete amounts, use,

Basement sq ft_____

Garage sq ft_____

Porch sq ft_____

Driveway sq ft_____

To determine plywood or OSB subfloor amounts and drywall amounts for ceilings, use,
(use second floor sq. ft. to determine attic insulation)

First Floor sq ft_____

Second Floor sq ft_____

Other Floors sq ft _____

To determine roofing materials needed use calculated sq. ft.

Roof #1 sq ft_____

Roof #2 sq ft_____

Roof #3 sq ft_____

Converting linier and square footages to material quantities

With the key measurements in hand, it is easy to determine the amount of materials needed. Use the formula and instructions that follow and refer to the cross sections on your blueprints to answer nomenclature questions and for depictions of how the materials fit together.

Material calculations have been broken down into common large lumber loads. Combine actual delivery loads as needed

LOAD ONE SUPPORTS and BASEMENT FRAME WALLS
(Beams and supports, exterior and interior basement frame walls, floor joists, plywood or OSB subfloor, blocking and bracing)

First Floor supports and joists
Basement beams and posts, wood and steel, needed to support first floor joist system. See the foundation plan. Count these Items individually.

Rolls of Sill Sealer
(use key linier feet)

Basement Exterior Walls total linear ft divided by length of a roll, (get on-line) equals number of rolls, (roll widths vary, select to fit width of sill plates, double if needed)

Treated Sill Plates
(use key linier feet)

Total linear ft of basement exterior walls divided by 16 (plus a few) equals number of treated 2"x8" or 2"x10"x16' treated plates needed. (See blueprint cross sections). (Lengths longer than 16' are expensive and unnecessary).

Note:
Include lumber needed for basement frame walls in this load, (Load One). Use key linier feet and methods outlined below to calculate basement frame walls. Basement exterior frame walls are support walls and must be in-place to walls.

Note:
*Exterior wall Studs are specified as 2"x4"or 2"x6".
*Basement wall studs may also be 2"x8"
*Interior walls are normally 2"x4" but basement support walls may also be *2"x6". Wall heights can be 8', 9' or higher. Separate wall lengths by height
*A (precut stud) is a stud cut short so when a bottom plate and two top plates are applied the ceiling height will be 8' or 9'.
*Wall Studs are spaced at 16" on center to accommodate the nailing of 4' by 8' drywall sheets and exterior wall sheathing.
*Exterior and interior walls use many extra studs at corners, where walls connect, and at windows and door openings,. Rather than counting extra studs, estimate the entire wall with studs at 12" on center, (instead of 16" on center), and your estimate will be very close. Simply use the total linier feet as the number of studs required.

Note:

Wall top and bottom plates are long 2"x4" or 2"x6" boards nailed to the bottom and top of stud to make a box. This is normally done while the wall section is laying flat on the new subfloor. When the studs are in place, the wall section is stood-up, moved into place, checked for level, and nailed to the subfloor. A second top plate is then added to tie the wall sections together. Three plates are needed for each wall section, one bottom, and two top plates.

Basement *Exterior Walls* Top and Bottom Wall Plates
(Use key linier feet)

Multiply total linear ft of basement exterior walls by 3, then divided by 16 to determine the number of 2x4, 2x6 or 2x8 x 16' plates needed for *two* top and *one* bottom plate. (Add 10% for backing, and waste)

Basement *Interior Walls*, Top and Bottom Wall Plates
(Use key linier feet)

Multiply total linear ft of basement interior walls by 3 then divided by 16 to determine the number of 2x4 or 2x6 x 16' plates needed for two top and one bottom plate. *(Add 10% for bracing and backing)*

Basement Exterior Frame Walls, Studs Needed
(Use key linier feet)

The number of 2x4 / 2x6 / 2x8 wall studs needed is the same as the linier feet of basement exterior frame walls

Basement Interior Frame Walls, Studs Needed
(Use key linier feet)

The number of 2x4 or 2x6 wall studs needed for basement interior walls is the same as the linier feet of basement interior walls.

Note:

Wall openings for doors and windows need a structural member above the opening to support weight from floors or roofs above. To keep pricing simple, (unless LVLs are specified), assume all headers to be 2x12s with ½" plywood spacers glued between.

Basement Exterior and Interior Frame Wall Headers 2X12s & plywood needed
(Use key linier feet from above)

Use the total length of basement wall openings, in both exterior and interior walls. Double the total amount, and divide by 16 to get the number of 2x12x16' boards needed. Add

15% for waste and overlap. Add 1 sheet of 4x8 cdx plywood for every (4) 2X12s. Add one case of construction glue.

Special Basement Headers

Large openings in basement Walls, both exterior and interior, may require special beams or headers known as LVLs, (Laminated Vaneer Lumber). These are specified on the floor plans. Count and list each type or size separately.

LOAD TWO FIRST FLOOR DECK

Joists and rim joists, plywood or OSB subfloor, blocking and bracing.

Note:

First Floor joists are indicated on the Basement plan by a long arrow with arrowheads on both ends and a notation like: 2" X 10" @ 16" OC over. This indicates that the subfloor above is to rest on 2" X 10" joists spaced at 16" center to center. The direction of the arrow indicates the direction of the floor joists above. Lumber comes in 2' lengths, (14', 16' 18' etc). Depending on the species of lumber, single 2 X 10s @ 16" OC can normally span no more than 15'-4". Floor joists are strengthened when the subfloor is glued and nailed to the joists and when drywall is applied below. Rim joists are joists nailed to the ends of floor joists to make the box that stabilizes the joists and supports exterior frame walls above.

First Floor Joists (Use the instructions below and the blueprints to measure and determine the number of joists needed).

On the basement floor plan, locate the two-headed arrows and the annotations indicating the size, direction, and spacing of the floor joists above. These double-headed arrows indicate which direction the joists will run to support the floor. To determine the length of the joists, measure from the outside of the exterior wall the arrow is pointing at to center of the beam or to the outside of the opposite exterior wall. To determine the total number of joist needed measure from the outside walls to the opposite outside walls that run parallel to the arrows. For 16" on center joists, multiply the length measured by 0.833. Repeat the process for each separate row of joists. Add 15% for scrap and to use as blocking between joists and for rim joists. Add any double or extra joists indicated on the drawings.

First Floor Sub Floor Materials
(use key square footage)

The square ft. of the first floor divided by 32 equals the number of ¾" T & G (tongue and groove) plywood or the number of sheets of OSB needed to cover the first floor joists. For waste, add 1 more sheet for every 10 calculated. Include a case of quart sized sub floor glue for every 16 sheets.

LOAD THREE FIRST FLOOR WALLS

Wall plates, studs, headers, sheathing

First Floor *Exterior Frame Walls*, Top and Bottom Wall Plates
(Use key linier feet)

Multiply total linear ft of First Floor exterior walls by 3, then divided by 16 to determine the number of 2x4 or 2x6 x 16' plates needed for *two* top and *one* bottom plate. (Add 10% for backing, and waste)

First Floor *Interior Frame Walls*, Top and Bottom Wall Plates
(Use key linier feet)

Multiply total linear ft of First Floor interior walls by 3 then divided by 16 to determine the number of 2x4 x 16' plates needed for two top and one bottom plate. *(Add 25% for bracing and backing)*

First Floor *Exterior Frame Walls*, Studs
(Use key linier feet)

Linier feet of exterior walls equals the number of 2x4 or 2x6 wall studs needed for First Floor exterior walls. Separate walls with different heights.

First Floor *Interior Frame Walls*, Studs
(Use key linier feet)

Linier feet of interior walls, equals the number of 2x4 wall studs needed for First Floor interior walls. Separate walls with different heights.

Note:

Wall openings for doors and windows need a structural member above the opening to support weight from floors or roofs above. To keep pricing simple assume these structural members to be 2x12s with ½" plywood spacers glued between.

First Floor *exterior and Interior Frame Wall*, Headers
(Use key linier feet from above)

Use the total length of First Floor wall openings in both exterior and interior walls. Double the total amount for 2"X4" walls, Triple the amount for 2"X6" walls, and divide by 16 to get the number of 2x12x16' boards needed. Add 10% for waste. Add 1 sheet of 4x8 cdx plywood for every 3 boards. Add two cases of construction glue.

Special First Floor Headers

Large openings in First Floor Walls, both exterior and interior, may require special beams or headers known as LVLs, (Laminated Vaneer Lumber). These are specified on floor plans. Count and list them separately

Note:

Wall sheathing, nailed to the outside of the exterior walls, provides strength and a nailing surface for siding. See cross-sections on your blueprints for the type specified. Sheathing comes in 4x8 sheets. Add extra material for walls over 8' high and note that structural sheathing must overlap joists and plates to tie walls to the foundation and to walls below.

First Floor, Exterior Wall Sheathing
(use key linier feet)

Divide linier feet of First Floor exterior walls by 4 to determine the number of 4' X 8' sheets of sheathing, (plywood, OSB, or insulated). Add 2 sheets for every outside or inside corner of the house. Add extra sheets for structural overlaps and for walls over 8' tall.

LOAD *FOUR SECOND* FLOOR DECK
Joists, sub floor materials, wall plates, wall studs, wall sheathing

Second Floor Joists (use first floor instructions with second floor measurements to determine the number of joists needed)

Second Floor Sub Floor Materials (use first floor instructions with second floor square footages to determine number of 4'X8' sheets needed)

LOAD FIVE SECOND FLOOR WALLS

Second Floor *Exterior Frame Walls,* Top and Bottom Wall Plates
(Use first floor instructions with second floor measurements)

Second Floor *Interior Frame Walls,* Top and Bottom Wall Plates
(Use first floor instructions with second floor measurements)

Second Floor *Exterior Frame Walls,* Studs
(Use first floor instructions with second floor measurements)

Second Floor *Interior Frame Walls,* Studs
(Use first floor instructions with second floor measurements)

Second Floor *exterior and Interior Frame Wall,* Headers
(Use first floor instructions with second floor measurements)

Special Second Floor wall Headers
(Use first floor instructions with second floor measurements)

Second Floor, Exterior Wall Sheathing
(Use first floor instructions with second floor measurements)

LOAD SIX ROOF FRAMING AND SHEATHING MATERIALS

Note:
Roof trusses placed at 24" o.c. are covered with 4' X 8' sheets of 5/8" plywood or OSB, (see cross section details on the blueprints). Order the roof sheathing with this load, along with needed ties and clips, so they are on site when the trusses arrive. Some dimensioned lumber is also required for trussed roofs. 2'x6' boards are needed for fascia to hold rain gutters, 2'X4' boards for outlooks to hold the soffit, and 2'X6' and 2'X8' boards to build rakes and for trim. See your blueprints cross sections for details.

Roof Sheathing, 4'X8' OSB sheets
Divide the total square feet of roof (from key dimensions above), by 32 to determine the number of 4 X 8 sheets needed. Add 1 sheet for every eight calculated for waste

Miscellaneous Roof Framing Lumber
Use the key linear measurements, width and slope distance, you used to determine square footage for the roof. Multiply the total of all key roof width linear measurements by 2 and divide by 16 to get the 2 X 6 X 16' boards needed for gutters and the number of 2 X 4 X 16' boards needed for outlooks. Multiply the total of all roof slope linier distances by 2 and divide by 16 to get the number of 2 X 6 X 16' boards and the number of 2 X 8 X 16' boards needed for rakes and trim. Add for waste.

Fasteners, Ties, Straps and Clips
Your framing crew will need special ties to connect the roof trusses to the walls and may need other straps and clips to fasten the first floor to the basement, the second floor to the first, and small "H" clips to keep the plywood or OSB roof sheathing separated a fraction of an inch to prevent moisture damage.

Provide (4) "H" clips for every sheet of plywood or OSB you calculated for roof sheathing, order ½" clips for ½" sheathing, 5/8" clips for 5/8" sheathing etc.

Provide (2) truss ties for each truss plus extras.
Ask the framers if they need straps or other ties to meet codes. See blueprints.

LOAD SEVEN MANUFACTURED ROOF TRUSSES

Most new homes use engineered roof trusses. Truss package prices include delivery but prices are normally not directly available to Home Owners. Lumber companies include the truss package price in their total lumber package price. Big Box Home Improvement Stores may be able to get a separate delivered price but will include their own mark up. Coordinating the delivery with a crane and the framing crew may be difficult.

LOAD EIGHT ROOFING MATERIALS

Note:

Roofing material estimates are in "squares", (10' X 10') or (100 square foot units). Your key measurements include the square feet of roof. Divide the key square feet by 100 and you have the squares you need of felt, and shingles.

Roofing felt comes in (two) thicknesses, #15 and #30, each cover a different area. One roll of #15 felt covers 432 sq ft, #30 felt covers 216 sq ft.

Roof Ice guard is a heavy polypropylene product that prevents ice damage along the edges of the roof. It comes in rolls of different lengths, usually 50' X 3'. A 3' wide strip along all roof edges is common.

Roof shingles are sold in bundles with different year warranties, (the heavier the shingle the longer the warranty). A bundle of heavy, "40 year" shingles covers fewer squares than a thinner, "30 year" shingle. Shake and metal roofing also covers different numbers of squares. The products are complicated but calculating what you need is simple.

Rolls of Felt
Divide the total square feet of roof by the square feet in each roll. Add several rolls to allow for overlap and waste.

Ice Guard
Use the total linier feet of both roof width and slope divided by the length of a roll of ice guard to determine how many rolls are needed.

Ridge Vent

Use your blueprints, measure the total ridgeline of your roof to determine how much ridge vent you need. Ridge vent comes in rolls and in shorter solid pieces. Look on-line.

Valley Flashing

Measure the flat length of valley on the roof plan. Multiply by the appropriate slope factor for calculating a hip roof, (located above in key quantities). Divide the total valley length by the length of a preformed valley-flashing piece, usually 12', or by the length of a roll of flashing.

Drip Edge

Refer to the key dimensions above for the total length of roof width and slope. Divide the total by the length of one piece of preformed drip edge, usually 10'.

Shingles, Shakes, Metal Roofing

Choose the shingle manufacture, type and coverage. Multiply the number of squares, (100 sq. ft.) of roof by the number of bundles per square to determine the number of bundles. Add bundles for waste and for later repairs. Don't come up short.

Example: 2,500 square feet of roof equals 25 squares of roof. At three bundles needed to cover one square, 75 bundles + extras are needed.

LOAD NINE WINDOWS AND SLIDING GLASS DOORS

Type, sizes, style, and manufacture is specified on the blueprints. You need to select color and accessories. A total delivered price should be available from your supplier.

LOAD TEN INSULATION MATERIALS

Use the key square footages of exterior walls, and ceilings below attic spaces to determine your insulation needs. Additional insulation for basement walls, joist pockets, and air infiltration points are secondary requirements. Foam sealant around windows, exterior doors, pipes wires etc. is essential, especially, if your house must pass a pressure test.

Joist pocket insulation
Basement joist pockets and second floor joist pockets are the areas between the end of floor joists and around the side of floor joists where lumber is exposed directly to the outside. Estimate these areas using rolls of R-30 paper faced insulation. Cut the rolls into pieces to fit between joists and into sidewall areas. Paper faces inward. Divide the total perimeter linier feet of exterior basement and first floor walls, (if a two story house), by the length of the R-30 rolls and divide by (2) to determine the insulation needed.

Basement wall insulation
Use the total perimeter linier feet of exterior basement wall to determine blanket insulation needs. If the basement walls have studs or have had studs added, determine the rolls of insulation needed to fit between studs by selecting a faced R-13 insulation of the correct width to fit between the studs and divide the total perimeter footage by the width of the insulation. Multiply the result by the height of the basement wall to determine the total linier feet of R-13 insulation needed. Divide by the length of the R-13 roll to determine the number of rolls needed.

Foam sealant insulation
For a price estimate, price a case of small cans of foam insulation available at a home improvement store. Use caution when sealing around windows and doors. Foam expansion can push window and doorframes out of alignment and cause problems. Use minimally expansive foam in these areas. Foam around wall sockets and plumbing in exterior walls.

Exterior wall insulation
Determine exterior wall requirements by referring to the blueprints and heat loss submissions for the type and "R" value specified. Estimating full cavity foam applications

is not easy. To keep it simple, estimate using 16" faced batten insulation similar to the "R" value specified for foam. Using the key square footage of the exterior walls, divide by the coverage per roll of insulation to determine the number of rolls of insulation needed. Use the same procedure for first and second floors.

Ceiling insulation

Insulating between floors, with the exception of rooms over unheated spaces like a garage, is unnecessary. Ceilings with unheated space above, such as attics, require substantial insulation. Estimate blown insulation material costs is difficult, so estimate using batten insulation of a similar "R" value to that specified for the blown insulation. Divide the square footage of the ceiling to be insulated, (same as the square footage of the floor below), by the coverage per roll to determine the number of rolls needed. Include enough cardboard vent blocks to keep insulation from blocking airflow into the attic at the ends of trusses.

LOAD ELEVEN DRYWALL
(Drywall, drywall compound, tape)

Knowing the approximate cost of the materials will allow you to evaluate bids, but for a whole house project, a drywall contractor that provides both labor and materials is best. For convenience, break the material calculations into drywall needed per floor, (finished lower level, garage, first floor, second floor and attic rooms). Disregard wall openings when estimating.

!/2" drywall is adequate over 16" on center framing, (walls and floor joists). **5/8"** Drywall is required for 24" on center framing as on ceilings under roof trusses.

Drywall for exterior walls
Use the key dimensions you calculated previously. For exterior walls, multiply the total linier feet of wall by the wall height to determine the square feet of drywall needed. Disregard the wall openings. For pricing estimating purposes, assume the use of 4' X 8' sheets only. Divide the square feet of exterior walls, (walls needing drywall on one side only), by 32 to get the number of ½"- 4 X 8 sheets needed, (add 10% for waste).

Drywall for interior walls
For interior walls multiply the total linier feet of walls by the wall height and double the amount, (drywall is on both sides of interior walls), Divide the square foot total by 32 to determine the number of ½"- 4 X 8 sheets of drywall needed, (add 10% for waste).

Drywall for ceilings with 16" on center framing
Use the key square footage calculated previously for the floor below ceilings that need ½" drywall, (finished basement rooms, first floor, etc). Divide by 32 to get the number of ½"- 4 X 8 sheets of drywall needed, (add 10% for waste).

Drywall for ceilings with 24" on center framing
Use the key square footage calculated previously for the floor below ceilings that need 5/8" drywall, (second floor, attic rooms, etc). Divide by 32 to get the number of 5/8"- 4 X 8 sheets of drywall needed, (add 10% for waste)

Drywall compound, tape etc
For pricing purposes, add a few hundred dollars per floor for compound, tape etc.

LOAD TWELVE INTERIOR DOORS AND TRIM MATERIALS
(stairs, baseboards, crown, jambs, railings, chair-rail)

Trim materials

Notes
Some trim materials are priced by the linier foot. Others are priced as precut lengths. Calculate the total linier feet needed per room or for an entire floor, (first floor, second floor etc).

Trim comes pre-painted, (usually white), pre-stained, and unstained. Trim also comes in different wood species, in many different profiles, and with prices from reasonable to very expensive. A common trim stain shade or paint color for the entire house makes decorating easier. Use a more decorative profile to accent formal rooms.

Use the key dimensions above for wall openings. Key dimensions were divided into exterior wall openings and interior wall openings because, like drywall, trim is applied to both sides of interior walls and only one side of exterior walls.

Stairs
If stairs are to be closed, (solid risers under each tread with stringers blocking both sides), and are to be carpeted, estimate using less expensive poplar treads. Note the width of the stairs on your blueprints, count the number of treads shown, and look up poplar stair tread and riser prices on line. Home improvement stores carry stair treads and risers in 3' and 4' lengths. Don't forget basement stairs.

If stairs are to ne stained, look up oak treads and riser prices.
For pull-down stairs for the garage or attic note the ceiling height and price on line.
For curved or pre-built stairs, the builder/manufacture will have prices.

Railings
Railings and balusters come in soft and hard wood, and in many styles. For a quick estimate, (if not available from the manufacture or supplier), estimate the linier feet needed from the blueprints and price the rail and base by the linier foot and estimate the number of balusters needed by multiplying the total rail length by four.

Exterior door and window jambs
Use the key dimensions above for basement, first floor and second floor wall-opening widths and window heights.

To estimate the linier feet of window jambs needed, add the total linier feet of wall opening widths to the total number of feet of window opening heights and double the result. Because door bottoms and windowsills will be excluded, the total will be an overestimate. Keep the overestimate as a pad for waste.

Windowsills
If windowsills are simple boards, disregard pricing them. If they are marble or another special material, price by using the key linier feet of wall of exterior wall openings.

Interior doorjambs
Count the number of interior wall openings. Doors average seven feet in height. Multiply the number of interior wall openings by eight, add the total linier feet of wall openings and double the result. Because door bottoms will be excluded, the total will be an over estimate. Keep the over estimate as a pad for waste. Use piece prices or linier foot prices to determine an estimate

Baseboard
Use the key wall length measurements to determine the amount of baseboard needed. Ignore door openings to allow for waste. Exterior walls need base on only one side. Interior walls need base on both sides, double the wall lengths for base needed on interior walls.

Crown molding and chair-rail
There is no, previously measured, key footage amounts for these trim items. Measure each room separately for the linier feet of crown molding or chair rail needed. Allow for waste.

LOAD THIRTEEN ENTRY DOORS

Sizes and handing, (which way the door swings), is specified on your blueprints. You need to select style, type, and manufacture. You also need to select type, style, finish and manufacture of entry door locksets. For fancy doors and locksets, order early.

OTHER LOADS

Gravel
Under slabs, driveways,
Gravel is priced by the ton and comes by the truckload. Your excavator and the gravel supplier will be the best sources of how many tons and types of gravel needed for the basement, the driveway, for backfill over footer drains, etc.

Concrete
(house slab floors, garage floor, basement floor, driveway, patios, sidewalks)

Concrete comes in different strengths for different purposes. Ask your local concrete ready mix company for advice when you get cubic yard prices. Concrete is priced and ordered by the cubic yard. Estimating in cubic yards is easy when a concrete slabs thickness in inches is converted into a percentage of a foot.

For example, 2" =.166' 4"=.333' 6" =.5' 8" =.666'

To determine the cubic yards of concrete needed, multiply the square feet of concrete needed by the decimal equivalent above and divide by 27.

END